100 DSM-5 Quest: Worker Should Know

ASWB®-LCSW Exam Preparation Guide

100 DSM-5 Questions Every Social Worker Should Know

ASWB®-LCSW Exam Preparation Guide

Harvey Norris, MSW, LCSW

TURTLE PRESS

©2016 Harvey Norris, MSW, LCSW
Turtle Press

All Rights Reserved
No Part of this book may be reproduced, stored in a retrieval system, or transmitted, in any form or by any means without written permission of the author.

Printed in the USA

ISBN-13: 978-1534660403
ISBN-10: 1534660402

Library of Congress Cataloging in Publication Data

Norris, Harvey S.

Dedication

This book is dedicated to my Father. Born in 1940, he was raised in a world and seen things which future generations will only know from the pages of dusty books and old blogs. Still he was able to instill in me values and morals which have allowed me to pursue my dreams and not be pushed aside or loose my path.

"Determine what you stand for, mark a circle around it (in your mind) and then defend it to your death. Never let anyone take it away."

Davis Scott Norris, December 1, 1940 –

FAIR USE ASSERTION

Any materials used in this book to illustrate and assist in comprehension, have been used under the Fair Use Copyright assertion of Section 107

Section 107 contains a list of the various purposes for which the reproduction of a particular work may be considered fair, such as criticism, comment, news reporting, teaching, scholarship, and research. Section 107 also sets out four factors to be considered in determining whether or not a particular use is fair:

- The purpose and character of the use, including whether such use is of commercial nature or is for nonprofit educational purposes
- The nature of the copyrighted work
- The amount and substantiality of the portion used in relation to the copyrighted work as a whole
- The effect of the use upon the potential market for, or value of, the copyrighted work

The distinction between fair use and infringement may be unclear and not easily defined. There is no specific number of words, lines, or notes that may safely be taken without permission. Acknowledging the source of the copyrighted material does not substitute for obtaining permission.

The 1961 Report of the Register of Copyrights on the General Revision of the U.S. Copyright Law cites examples of activities that courts have regarded as fair use: "quotation of excerpts in a review or criticism for purposes of illustration or comment; quotation of short passages in a scholarly or technical work, for illustration or clarification of the author's observations; use in a parody of some of the content of the work parodied; summary of an address or article, with brief quotations, in a news report; reproduction by a library of a portion of a work to replace part of a damaged copy; reproduction by a teacher or student of a small part of a work to illustrate a lesson; reproduction of a work in legislative or judicial proceedings or reports; incidental and fortuitous reproduction, in a newsreel or broadcast, of a work located in the scene of an event being reported. "Copyright protects the particular way authors have expressed themselves. It does not extend to any ideas, systems, or factual information conveyed in a work.

This work and MyMSW.info are not affiliated with or endorsed by ASWB

2015 Edition

200 Questions Every Social Worker Should Know

www.MyMSW.info

LCSW Exam Prep

Harvey Norris, LCSW

www.MyMSW.info presents...

Psychotherapist's
FLASH CARD BOOK

12 Personality Theorists

404 FLASH CARDS

ASWB - LCSW
EXAM STUDY
MATERIAL

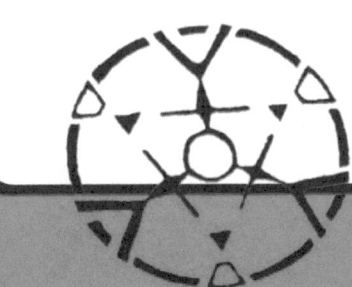

Psychotherapist's FLASH CARD BOOK

Harvey Norris

www.MyMSW.info
Presents

Social Work Glossary

Edited by
Harvey Norris, LCSW

The MyMSW
Field Guide Series

DSM5 - Question 1
According to the DSM 5, when you are evaluating a client and they present with abnormalities in one or more of the following 5 domains: delusions, hallucinations, disorganized thinking, abnormal motor behavior and negative symptoms, the BEST general diagnosis is... **[ANSWER: Page 61]**

A) Schizophreniform Disorder
B) Brief Psychotic Disorder
C) Schizophrenia Spectrum Disorder
D) Schizotypal Disorder

DSM5 - Question 2
According to the DSM 5, patients showing signs of Alogia and Anhedonia are displaying which of the Key Features that define Psychotic Disorders... **[ANSWER: Page 61]**
A) Hallucinations
B) Negative Symptoms
C) Delusions
D) Disorganized Thinking

DSM5 - Question 3
According to the DSM 5, you are working with a patient who believes that an unknown entity has been removing thoughts from their head during the day and putting thoughts in their head at night. Which of the 5 key features that define psychosis are at play here... **[ANSWER: Page 62]**

A) Hallucinations
B) Delusions
C) Grossly Disordered Behavior
D) Negative Symptoms.

DSM5 - Question 4

According to the DSM 5, the Negative symptom of Avolition is defined as... **[ANSWER: Page 63]**

A) decrease in motivated self-initiated purposeful activities.
B) an apparent lack of interest in social activity
C) decrease in the amount of speech output
D) a decrease in the ability to experience pleasure from a positive stimuli or a degradation in the recollection of a pleasure previously experienced

DSM5 - Question 5

According to the DSM 5, An individual presents to you with the following symptoms: They relate no major or manic episode, they have had a fixed belief they are being attacked by insects, despite the fact there is no physical evidence of infestation. They have believed this for the past 2 months. They have a minor hallucination that their skin itches because of these insects. They are attending work daily but are beginning to have difficulty paying attention to their job duties and they deny any history or current use of drugs. Their urine drug screen (UDS) is negative. Your BEST diagnosis would be... **[ANSWER: Page 63]**

A) Brief Psychotic Disorder
B) Schizophrenia
C) Schizophreniform Disorder
D) Delusional Disorder

DSM5 - Question 6

You are reviewing the intake paperwork on a client with the following documented symptoms: Markedly diminished interest in almost all activities for most of the day, nearly every day as indicated by family reports; self-reports of sleeping 13-14 hours per day; a general feeling of fatigue every day; problems with thinking or concentrating every day which is impacting their college classes; and recurrent suicidal ideation without a specific plan almost daily.

These symptoms have been present and observable for at least 3 weeks and there is no stated stressor event to indicate a trigger for this behavior pattern.

A review of the drug screen is positive for benzodiazepines, however, they were agitated during the intake and were given an intramuscular shot of Ativan. There is no self-report or family history which would indicate any glandular issues; e.g. hypothyroidism, etc. Your best diagnostic impression would be... **[ANSWER: Page 64]**

A) Major Depressive Disorder Recurrent
B) Major Depressive Episode
C) Disruptive Mood Dysregulation Disorder
D) Major Depressive Disorder with Mixed Features.

DSM5 - Question 7
Given the revisions in the DSM5, which of the following is NOT TRUE of Personality Disorders in general diagnosis. **[ANSWER: Page 66]**

A) Like the DSM-IV-TR, the personality disorders in the DSM5 are separated into three distinct clusters; A, B, & C.
B) Like the DSM-IV-TR, the personality disorders in the DSM5 represent the categorical perspective that personality disorders are qualitatively distinct clinical

syndromes.
C) Like the DSM-IV-TR, the personality disorders in the DSM5 are coded on AXIS II.
D) Like the DSM-IV-TR, the personality disorders in the DSM5 are defined as "an enduring pattern of inner experience and behavior that deviates markedly from the expectations of the individual's culture."

DSM5 - Question 8

You are reading a patient's chart and note that the patient has a diagnosis of Schizoid Personality Disorder. You immediately understand that this individual will show the following traits. **[ANSWER: Page 67]**

A) a pattern of grandiosity, need for admiration and a lack of empathy.
B) a pattern of instability in interpersonal relationships, self-image, and affects, and marked impulsivity.
C) a pattern of submissive and clinging behavior related to an excessive need to be taken care of.
D) a pattern of detachment from social relationships and a restricted range of emotional expression.

DSM5 - Question 9

In order to be diagnosed with a personality disorder the patient must meet 7 criteria. The first of these are an enduring pattern of inner experience and behavior that deviates markedly from the individual's culture. Which of the following is NOT a criterion for the diagnosis? **[Page 67]**

A) The enduring pattern is inflexible and pervasive across a broad range of personal and social situations.

B) The enduring pattern is attributable to the physiological effects of a substance (e.g. a drug of abuse, a medication) or another medical condition.
C) The enduring pattern leads to clinically significant distress or impairment in social, occupational or other important areas of functioning.
D) The pattern is stable and of long duration, and its onset can be traced back at least to adolescence or early childhood.

DSM5 - Question 10
Which of the following is a TRUE statement of the issues surrounding the differential diagnosis of a personality disorder? **[ANSWER: Page 68]**

A) When personality changes emerge and persist after an individual has been exposed to extreme stress, a diagnosis of post traumatic stress disorder should be considered.
B) While the behavior should generally not occur exclusively during the course of schizophrenia or a Bipolar Disorder, as long as the behavior causes clinically significant impairment, it can be used for the diagnosis
C) The defining characteristics can have appeared before early adulthood or later in the adult life cycle.
D) Personality traits which do not meet the threshold of inflexible, maladaptive, and persisting and cause significant functional impairment or subjective distress can be used in the diagnosis when appropriate.

DSM5 - Question 11
DSM–IV described two distinct disorders, alcohol abuse and alcohol dependence, in the DSM–5 the two disorders, into a single disorder called alcohol use disorder (AUD). Which of the following is not true of the new diagnostics?
[ANSWER: Page 69]

A) DSM–5 eliminates legal problems as a criterion.
B) DSM–5 adds craving as a criterion for an AUD diagnosis.
C) Under DSM–IV, the diagnostic criteria for abuse and dependence were identical:
D) Under DSM–5, anyone meeting any two of the 11 criteria during the same 12-month period would receive a diagnosis of AUD.

DSM5 - Question 12
Your client was diagnosed with an Alcohol Use Disorder, Mild, and was notable for criteria 1 (Alcohol taken in larger amounts or over a longer period than intended); Criteria 2 (There was a persistent desire or unsuccessful efforts to cut down or control alcohol use); and 4 (There was a craving or strong desire or urge to use alcohol). After five months in an Intensive Outpatient Program (IOP), where your client has remained alcohol-free, your client no longer experiences criteria 1 or 2, but still relates criteria 4. The appropriate modifier to use on this 6-month reassessment would be...
[ANSWER: Page 69]

A) in early remission.
B) in sustained remission.
C) in continual remission.

D) in a controlled environment.

DSM5 - Question 13
Which of the following are important characteristics of a Substance Use Disorder? [ANSWER: Page 70]

A) underlying changes in brain circuits may persist beyond detoxification, particularly in individuals with severe disorders.
B) The behavioral effects of the of these brain changes may be exhibited in repeated relapses and intense drug cravings.
C) Individuals exposed to drug-related stimuli may be more likely to relapse.
D) All of the above.

DSM5 - Question 14
The DSM5 has chosen to officially omit the word ADDICTION to describe more extreme presentations. Which of the following best describe this position…?
[ANSWER: Page 71]

A) The more neutral term of substance use disorder is used.
B) multiple cultures use the term differently and this creates uncertainty around its use and meaning.
C) it has a potentially negative connotation.
D) All of the above.

DSM5 - Question 15
Of the following clinically significant problematic behavioral or psychological changes attributed with intoxication, which is NOT included in the DSM5? [DSM5 Page 485]

[ANSWER: Page 71]

A) belligerence
B) driving under the influence
C) mood liability
D) impaired

DSM5 - Question 16
You have been asked to see a client who presents with the following symptoms: They are reporting feeling "detached from their body" and also feeling as if they are "detached from their surroundings." They relate feeling slightly anxious about this but more confused and embarrassed by their inability to understand why this is happening or when it started. However, after several questions you determine their reality testing is intact. Your best diagnostic guess would be... [ANSWER: Page 71]

A) Dissociative Identity Disorder 300.14 (F44.81)
B) Dissociative Amnesia 300.12 (F44.0)
C) Other Specified Dissociative Disorder 300.15 (F44.89)
D) Depersonalization/Derealization Disorder 300.6 (F48.1)

DSM5 - Question 17
Your client is diagnosed with a Depersonalization-Derealization Disorder 300.6 and has made statements including; "I am no one."; "I know I have feelings but I don't feel them."; and "I feel like I am having a 'out-of-the-body' experience." Of the following statements about the prevalence of this disorder in the general population, which is NOT TRUE? [ANSWER: Page 72]

A) Transient symptoms lasting for hours to days are common in the general population
B) Approximately 50% of all adults could be diagnosed with this disorder.
C) Lifetime diagnostic prevalence in in both US and Non-US populations is about 2%.
D) The breakdown between men and women with this disorder is 50%

DSM5 - Question 18

Over 70% of outpatients with _____ have attempted suicide. Multiple suicide attempts are common and self-directed violence is also common. Assessment of suicide risk is complicated when there is amnesia for past suicidal behaviors. This BEST described the risk of Suicide with which of the following disorders? **[ANSWER: Page 73]**

A) Dissociative Amnesia 300.12 (F44.0)
B) Depersonalization/Derealization Disorder 300.6 (F48.1)
C) Unspecified Dissociative Disorder 300.15 (F44.9)
D) Dissociative Identity Disorder 300.14 (F44.81)

DSM5 - Question 19

Individuals with Dissociative Amnesia may show multiple symptoms associated with other disorders. The DSM is designed to help you diagnose differentially, which means "screening out" other disorders with similar features. Your client presents with rigidity, posturing and an extremely flat affect, but is able to recall information upon questioning. This would tend to indicate that, rather than Dissociative Amnesia, the individual is showing signs of … **[ANSWER: Page 73]**

A) Post-traumatic amnesia due to brain injury
B) Catatonic stupor
C) Neurocognitive disorder
D) Seizure disorder

DSM5 - Question 20
When interacting with the client with dissociative amnesia, which of the following risk and prognostic factors are not accurate. [ANSWER: Page 74]

A) Single or repeated traumatic experiences such as war childhood maltreatment and natural disasters are common antecedents.
B) There is a definite link in the genetic studies between family members with dissociative amnesia.
C) Removal from the dramatic circumstances that underlie a dissociative amnesia, such as combat, may facilitate a rapid return of memory which may include an onset of post dramatic stress disorder symptoms.
D) the greater number of adverse childhood experiences, especially those dealing with physical or sexual abuse, interpersonal violence, or which are very severe frequent and violent, increases the risk of dissociative amnesia.

DSM5 - Question 21
When working with a client who has been diagnosed with Post Traumatic Stress Disorder (PTSD) 309.81 [F43.10], The risk and protective factors are generally broken into three temporal dimensions. Which of the following is NOT one of these dimensions? [ANSWER: Page 75]

A) Pretraumatic
B) Preceptortraumatic
C) Peritraumatic
D) Posttraumatic

DSM5 - Question 22

Diagnosing PTSD requires working through 8 different criteria. The first set, known as Criteria A specifically deal with "Exposure to actual or threatened death, serious injury, or sexual violence in one (or more) of the following ways." [DSM5 Page 271] Which of the following is not part of this criteria set? [ANSWER: Page 76]

A) Directly experiencing the traumatic events
B) Witnessing, in person the events as it occurs to others.
C) Learning that the traumatic events occurred to a close family member or close friend.
D) Exposure to violence through electronic media, television movies or pictures.

DSM5 - Question 23

The diagnostic criteria (B) in Post Traumatic Stress Disorder encapsulates intrusive symptoms associated with Traumatic events, beginning after the traumatic event occurs. Which of the following meet this criterion? [ANSWER: Page 76]

A) Intense psychological distress at exposure to cues which resemble and aspect of the event.
B) recurrent dreams and nightmares in which the content is related to the trauma
C) Dissociative reactions or flashbacks, where the clienteles as if the event is occurring.

D) All of the above

DSM5 - Question 24
The diagnostic criteria (D) in Post Traumatic Stress Disorder states "Negative alterations in cognitions and mood associated with the traumatic event(s) beginning or worsening after the traumatic event(s) occurred..." [Page 271]. Which of the following situations experienced by a Veteran who served in Iraq, might elicit a response which meets this criteria? [ANSWER: Page 77]

A) Driving by a car abandoned on the side of the road.
B) seeing a young man standing on a street corner.
C) Seeing a large dead animal near the roadway.
D) A & C

DSM5 - Question 25
You are working with a client who presents with the following features: Irritable behavior, angry outbursts, hyper vigilance, exaggerated startle response and problems concentrating. When questioned about PTSD, they state they have never experienced any trauma. Which of the following specifiers would you be likely to use? [ANSWER: Page 78]

A) with dissociative symptoms
B) with dissociative symptoms: Depersonalization
C) with dissociative symptoms: Derealization
D) with delated expression

DSM5 - Question 26
Food avoidance or restriction associated with the insufficient intake of food or the lack of interest in eating most commonly

develops in infancy or early childhood and may persist until the person is an adult. If this pattern continues the individual may develop an eating disorder. The diagnostic criteria for anorexia nervosa does not include which of the following criteria. **[ANSWER: Page 78]**

A) restriction of food intake leading to a significantly low bodyweight given age, sex, and developmental trajectory.
B) recurrent and inappropriate compensatory behaviors in order to prevent weight gain such as self induced vomiting, laxatives, and other medications.
C) a disturbance in the way one views the bodyweight shape with a persistent lack of recognition of the seriousness of the current low bodyweight.
D) intense fear of gaining weight or becoming fat with persistent behavior, even though they are significantly underweight.

DSM5 - Question 27

The DSM 5 lists three specific risk and prognostic factors for anorexia nervosa. These are the temperamental, the environmental, and genetic and physiological. Which of the following features is considered one of the temperamental risk and prognostic factors? **[ANSWER: Page 79]**

A) individuals who develop anxiety disorders or display obsessional traits in childhood have an increased risk of developing anorexia nervosa.
B) prevalence of anorexia nervosa is appropriate given the association with culture and societal norms in which thinness is valued.

C) if you have a first-degree biological relative with anorexia nervosa, you are more likely to have the disorder yourself.
D) concordance rates for anorexia nervosa in monozygotic twins are significantly higher than those of dizygotic twins.

DSM5 - Question 28
According to the DSM 5, a rumination disorder (307.53) is defined by the following four criteria. Of these criteria, which one is not described accurately? **[ANSWER: Page 79]**

A) repeated regurgitation of food over a period of at least one month with regurgitated food being re-chewed, re-swallowed, or spit out.
B) the repeated regurgitation is not attributed to a gastrointestinal or other medical condition.
C) the eating disturbance occurs exclusively during the course of anorexia nervosa, bulimia nervosa, a binge eating disorder, or avoidant/restrictive food intake disorder.
D) if the symptoms occur in the context of another mental disorder or neurological disorder then the symptoms are sufficiently severe to warrant additional clinical attention.

DSM5 - Question 29
According to the DSM5, Page 345, Bulimia Nervosa includes recurrent episodes of binge eating, recurrent inappropriate behaviors compensating for this binging which include self-induced vomiting, misuse of laxative or diuretics and excessive exercise, coupled with a self-evaluation which is

heavily influenced by body shape and weight. This behavior happens at least once a week for 3 months. Which of the following therapeutic issues are valid? [ANSWER: Page 80]

A) This disorder is far more common in females than males.
B) Suicide Risk is elevated in individuals with this disorder
C) Comorbid psychiatry disorders increase the likelihood of a worse long-term outcome.
D) All of the above

DSM5 - Question 30

Binge eating is defined as eating, in a discrete period of time, the amount of food that is definitely larger than most people would eat in a similar period of time under similar circumstances the DSM five defines the binge eating disorder (307.51) as a binge eating episode with a second characteristic. [Page 350]. This second characteristic is...
[ANSWER: Page 81]

A) eating large amounts of food when not feeling physically hungry.
B) the episodes of binge eating are not associated with recurrent compensatory behavior as seen in bulimia.
C) a sense of lack of control over eating occurs during the episode.
D) there is a feeling of being disgusted with oneself and guilty after the binge eating episodes

This is one of the five behaviors which comprise criteria B for the binge eating disorder. This is an important criterion to determine the extent of the binge eating disorder. However, this is not part of the initial two-pronged diagnostic criteria.

DSM5 - Question 31

Personality disorders in the DSM5 are defined as an enduring pattern of inner experience and behavior that deviates markedly from the expectations of the individual's culture, are pervasive and inflexible, and have an onset during adolescence or early adulthood, is stable over time, and leads to distress or impairment. The DSM5 uses the categorical approach, in which it considers each personality disorder to be a separate clinical syndrome. It lists 12 separate personality disorders. These disorders are further divided into three specific clusters. Cluster A includes the odd or eccentric disorders, Cluster B includes the dramatic, emotional or erratic personality disorders, and Cluster C includes the disorders which appear anxious or fearful. Of the following personality disorders below, which one does not fit into the Cluster C subcategory. **[ANSWER: Page 81]**

A) paranoid personality disorder
B) avoidant personality disorder
C) obsessive-compulsive personality disorder
D) dependent personality disorder

DSM5 - Question 32

According to the DSM5: in order to diagnose a personality disorder the clinician must have data which indicates an enduring pattern of inner experience and behavior that deviates markedly from the expectations of the individuals culture this pattern is manifested across at least two of the following dimensions of a patient's life. The first dimension is their cognition (or thought processes) which include their way of perceiving and interpreting themselves, other people and events. The second dimension is their affectivity (or

emotionality) which includes the range, intensity, lability, and appropriateness of emotional responses; their interpersonal functioning, which includes an understanding of how they interact with other people, and their impulse control. Data obtained from the 2001–2002 national epidemiological study on alcohol and related conditions suggests that the percentage of adults who have at least one personality disorder is approximately…
[ANSWER: Page 81]

A) 10%
B) 12%
C) 15%
D) 18%

DSM5 - Question 33

You have begun seeing a client who related several interactions with other people which appear odd. They stated that several days earlier they had ordered a large salad at a deli and were given small salad instead. They stated they became very angry with the clerk. When asked why they stated "They gave me a small salad because they think I am fat. " They also described an interaction with a coworker the previous day. The coworker remarked on how much they like the client's new boots. The coworker said the boots appeared expensive. The client stated he got mad at the coworker and said the coworker was trying to make fun of him because the coworker felt he could not forward the boots. When asked to describe his parents he described them as rigid and being unwilling to cooperate with other people. He stated they often blame everyone else for their problems. The personality disorder which matches his symptoms is…

[ANSWER: Page 83]

A) antisocial personality disorder
B) schizotypal personality
C) histrionic personality disorder
D) paranoid personality

DSM5 - Question 34
You have been asked to assess a 19-year-old male client who has involvement in the legal system involving at least two charges for battery. He has recently been charged with reckless driving, which occurred while he had his 18-year-old pregnant girlfriend in the car with him. He has given you two separate stories of the incident. and appears to lack remorse for his behavior. What would be the best possible diagnosis for this individual? [ANSWER: Page 84]

A) Schizotypal Personality Disorder
B) Antisocial Personality Disorder
C) Dependent Personality Disorder
D) Histrionic Personality Disorder

DSM5 - Question 35
You have been asked to evaluate a 24-year-old female who has just been terminated from her fourth job in 12 months. As she sits across from you you notice her dress and mannerisms are slightly odd and eccentric. She discusses her feelings and they appear metaphorical and over elaborate. She appears to endorse magical thinking and believes herself to be clairvoyant. She states she has a difficult time dealing with others because she has a "six sense" about them and how they will respond. Which of the personality disorders

should you be thinking about at this time during the assessment. **[ANSWER: Page 85]**

A) Schizotypal Personality Disorder
B) Antisocial Personality Disorder
C) Dependent Personality Disorder
D) Histrionic Personality Disorder

DSM5 - Question 36
You have been assessing a 22-year-old college student who just became a junior at the local State University. The first two years of their college career were spent at a community college and they lived at home. During the first semester at the University they have had three separate relationships. In each of the relationships they describe the individual as being great, perfect, and everything they were looking for. They stated that this lasts about three weeks and then they feel the person has changed and become someone they did not want to be around. They state that they hate being alone, and often feel like teachers don't like them, or wish them ill, when a teacher doesn't respond to them the way they think they should. They describe anxious moods that can last for eight hours to two or three days, but never longer. Which of the following is the best diagnosis for this individual?
[ANSWER: Page 85]

A) Borderline Personality Disorder
B) Antisocial Personality Disorder
C) Dependent Personality Disorder
D) Histrionic Personality Disorder

DSM5 - Question 37

You have begun to assess a 31-year-old client who has recently moved out from their parent's home. They described difficulty making decisions without having to call their parents and ask them questions several times. They state they often feel alone and helpless and wish they were in a relationship. The tell you they would like to be married in order to have somebody who can take care of them. they have related that when their brother says things to them they don't like, they have a difficult time disagreeing with them, because they fear their brother will no longer talk to them. What is the best possible diagnosis, of the following, for this individual?
[ANSWER: Page 86]

A) Schizotypal Personality Disorder
B) Antisocial Personality Disorder
C) Dependent Personality Disorder
D) Histrionic Personality Disorder

DSM5 - Question 38

You have begun assessing a 17-year-old child who expresses feeling inadequate and relates situations in which they appear to be hypersensitive to anybody talking negatively about them. They state they would prefer to spend their time at home and do not like to be around people. When asked about their schoolwork they state they enjoy school as long as they can do good in the class, however they often are concerned about being criticized for their work. When you ask them how they make new friends, it is clear they feel socially inept and inferior to others, and lack this skill set. Which of the following diagnoses would best fit this individual?
[ANSWER: Page 86]

A) paranoid personality disorder
B) avoidant personality disorder
C) obsessive-compulsive personality disorder
D) dependent personality disorder

DSM5 - Question 39
You have been referred a 36-year-old client who is very into fashion. They show up at your office in designer clothes, with designer shoes and at every opportunity during therapy, make comments about their dress and how you dress. Their language is very flowery, their expressions of emotion are exaggerated, and you often feel they could be described as, "over-the-top". When you ask how they interact with a large group of friends, they state to you, "as long as everyone listens to me, I'm great." Your best diagnosis for this individual would be?   [ANSWER: Page 87]

A) Schizotypal Personality Disorder
B) Antisocial Personality Disorder
C) Dependent Personality Disorder
D) Histrionic Personality Disorder

DSM5 - Question 40
You have begun working with a 42-year-old client. They were referred to you because their family feels they are depressed. The client states they have almost always lived alone, they enjoy going to work and they enjoy coming home and sitting in their apartment after work. When you ask about hobbies, they have none, and do not appear to be upset by this. When you ask them to identify one close friend they can call if they needed help, they are unable to provide a name or a phone

number. During the interview they endorse symptoms of a flat affect, low excitability, the a certain "emotional coldness." Your best possibility of a diagnosis is?
[ANSWER: Page 88]

A) Schizotypal Personality Disorder
B) Antisocial Personality Disorder
C) Dependent Personality Disorder
D) Schizoid Personality Disorder

DSM5 - Question 41
When you are diagnosing a personality disorder you need to separate out other disorders which may be similar in nature. Of the following four answers, three of them represent actual differential diagnosis issues. One is false.
[ANSWER: Page 88]

A) there is a great deal of overlap between avoidant personality disorder and social anxiety disorder, so much so that they may be alternative conceptualizations of the same or similar conditions. Avoidance also characterizes both avoidant personality disorders and Agoraphobia, and they often co-occur.
B) Narcissistic personality disorder must also be distinguished from symptoms that may develop in association with persistent substance use.
C) Histrionic personality disorder must be distinguished from personality change due to another medical condition in which the traits that emerge are attributable to the affects of another medical condition on the central nervous system.
D) Borderline personality disorder does not need to be

distinguished from symptoms that may develop in association with persistent substance use. The diagnosis of borderline personality disorder is exempt from differential diagnosis with substance use disorders.

DSM5 - Question 42
When diagnosing personality disorders it is important to review gender related diagnostic issues. Of the following gender related diagnostic issues, which one is false.
[ANSWER: Page 89]

A) borderline personality disorder is diagnosed predominantly in females, at a ratio of 3:1
B) schizoid personality disorder is diagnosed slightly more often in males and may cause more impairment in males.
C) schizotypal personality disorder may be slightly more common in females than in males.
D) in systematic studies, obsessive-compulsive personality disorder appears to be diagnosed about twice as often in males, at a ratio of 2:1.

DSM5 - Question 43
In the DSM5, the substance related disorders section encompasses 10 separate classes of drugs. These are alcohol, caffeine, cannabis, hallucinogens, inhalants, opioids, sedatives, hypnotics, and anxiolytics, stimulants, tobacco, and other unknown substances. Any of these substances may produce an intense activation of the brains neuro-chemical reward system which can cause maladaptive behaviors in normal activities of living. Of the following, which is an essential feature of a substance use disorder.

[ANSWER: Page 90]

A) a cluster of cognitive, behavioral, and physiological symptoms indicating that the individual continues using the substance despite significant substance related problems.
B) When using the substance there is an underlying change in brain neuro-circuits which may persist beyond detoxification. This is often seen as particularly prevalent in individuals with severe substance use disorders.
C) The behavioral effects of brain changes due to substance use maybe seen in the repeated relapses and intense drug cravings individual often show when being exposed to drug related stimuli.
D) all of the above.

DSM5 - Question 44

Please note: we no longer use the term dependence. These went away with the publication of DSM five. All substance use disorders are not listed by the name of the substance, abuse disorder, and severity.

Opioid use disorder needs to be diagnostically differentiated from severe alcohol intoxication. Opioid intoxication and alcohol intoxication present with similar symptoms and are often comorbid conditions. Of the following, which statement is not true regarding comorbidity of opioid use disorder. [ANSWER: Page 90]

A) Individuals with an opioid use disorder are at increased risk of developing mild to moderate depression which can meet the criteria for persistent depressive disorder

and in some cases major depressive disorder.
B) There are common medical conditions associated with opioid use disorder including HIV and hepatitis C. Both of these commonly occurring comorbid medical conditions are seen at equal prevalence rates between injection use and prescription abuse.
C) In opioid use disorder the individual may present with symptoms of slurred speech, attention impairment, memory impairment, and drowsiness.
D) Insomnia is common both in opioid use disorder and upon withdraw from opioid use.

DSM5 - Question 45

Opioid use disorder needs to be diagnostically differentiated from severe alcohol intoxication. Opioid intoxication and alcohol intoxication cannot only present with similar symptoms, they are often comorbid conditions. Of the following, which statement is not true regarding comorbidity of opioid use disorder. Please note: we no longer use the term dependence. This went away with the publication of DSM 5. All substance use disorders are not listed by the name of the substance, abuse disorder, and severity.
[ANSWER: Page 91]

A) individuals with an opioid use disorder are at increased risk of developing mild to moderate depression which can meet the criteria for persistent depressive disorder and in some cases major depressive disorder.
B) insomnia is common both in opioid use disorder and upon withdraw from opioid use.
C) in opioid use disorder the individual may present with symptoms of slurred speech, attention impairment,

memory impairment, and drowsiness.
D) there are common medical conditions associated with opioid use disorder including HIV and hepatitis C. Both of these commonly occurring comorbid medical conditions are seen at equal prevalence rates between injection use and prescription (pill) use.

DSM5 - Question 46
The DSM-V defines stimulant use disorder as a pattern of amphetamine-type substance, cocaine, or other stimulant use leading to clinically significant impairment or distress, as manifested by at least two of the following 11 criteria (page 561) occurring within a 12-month period. One of these criteria is tolerance to the stimulant used. Which of the following is/are correct regarding tolerance? [ANSWER: Page 92]

A) tolerance is a need for markedly increased amounts of the stimulant to achieve intoxication.
B) tolerance is an increase in the effect of the stimulant, while using the same amount.
C) tolerance is a markedly diminished effect with continued use of the same amount of the stimulant.
D) Both A and C

DSM5 - Question 47
There are five separate classes of alcohol related disorders. These include alcohol use disorder, alcohol intoxication, alcohol withdrawal, other alcohol induced disorders, and unspecified alcohol related disorder. When diagnosing an alcohol related disorder the client must show a "problematic pattern of alcohol use leading to clinically significant impairment or distress, as manifested by at least two of the

following, occurring within a 12-month period." Of the following criteria, which is an appropriate diagnostic for alcohol use disorder? **[ANSWER: Page 92]**

A) a great deal of time is spent in activities necessary to obtain alcohol, use alcohol, or recover from its effects.
B) important social, occupational, or recreational activities are given up or reduced because of alcohol use.
C) there is a persistent desire or unsuccessful efforts to cut down or control alcohol use.
D) all of the above.

DSM5 - Question 48

Alcohol use disorder, once diagnosed, generally requires the use of a specifier for severity. The specifier is as follows. Mild is the presence of 2 to 3 symptoms. Moderate is the presence of 4-5 symptoms. Severe is the presence of 6 or more symptoms. You are also able to specify whether or not remission is in a controlled environment, where access to alcohol is restricted, such as a treatment program, or incarceration.

The twelve-month prevalence rate of alcohol use disorder in the United States is 4.6% among 12 to 17-year-olds and 8.5% among adults aged 18 years or older. The rates breakdown among men and women as follows:12.4% for young adult men and 4.9% for adult women. Which of the following statements involving alcohol prevalence are true? [DSM Page 493]
[ANSWER: Page 93]

A) the twelve-month prevalence of alcohol use disorder among adults decreases in middle-age and is greatest

among individuals 18 to 29 years old and lowest among individuals for the 45 to 65 years old.
B) the twelve-month prevalence of alcohol use disorder among adults decreases in middle-age, and is greatest among individuals 18 to 29 years old and lowest among individuals for the 65 years old and older.
C) the twelve-month prevalence of alcohol use disorder among adults decreases in middle-age and is greatest among individuals 45 to 65 years old and lowest among individuals for the 65 years and older.
D) none of the above

DSM5 - Question 49

The essential features required in order to diagnose substance intoxication include: the development of a reversible substance specific syndrome due to the recent ingestion of a substance (criterion A). The clinically significant problematic behavioral or psychological changes associated with intoxication are attributable to the physiological effects of the substance on the central nervous system and they developed during or shortly after use of the substance (criterion B). The symptoms are not attributable to another medical condition and are not better explained by another mental disorder (criterion D). Which of the following are associated with Criterion B? **[ANSWER: Page 94]**

A) mood labiality
B) impaired judgment
C) belligerence
D) all of the above.

DSM5 - Question 50

Diagnostic markers related to persistent heavy use of alcohol include dyspepsia, nausea, bloating, gastritis, esophageal varices, hemorrhoids, unsteady gait, tremor, insomnia, and erectile dysfunction in males. Repeated heavy drinking in females is also associated with menstrual irregularities; and during pregnancy, spontaneous abortion and fetal alcohol syndrome. If the individual has a pre-existing history of seizures or head trauma they are more likely to develop alcohol related seizures. When withdrawing from alcohol the heavy user often experiences nausea, vomiting, gastritis, dry mouth, puffy blotchy complexion, and mild peripheral edema or swelling. Alcohol use disorder is also highly correlated with increased risk of accidents, violence, and suicide. Of the following, which is an accurate statement regarding the societal effects of alcohol use. **[ANSWER: Page 94]**

A) one in five intensive care unit in missions in urban hospitals is related to alcohol use.
B) 40% of individuals in the United States experience and alcohol related adverse event at sometime in their life
C) 55% of all fatal driving events include and are accounted for by alcohol use.
D) All of the above

DSM5 - Question 51

You been asked to evaluate a person who is presenting with the following features. They are belligerent, impulsive, unpredictable, they endorse psychomotor agitation, they have vertical Nystagmus, which means their eyes are moving in a rapid, uncontrolled, up-and-down motion. They exhibit a diminished response to pain, ataxia (a difficulty standing), muscle rigidity, and hypertension. They are unable to focus long enough to answer a number of questions. You suspect some type of substance intoxication. Given the symptoms, which substance intoxication is likely to be the best diagnosis. **[ANSWER: Page 95]**

A) Hallucinogen intoxication
B) amphetamine intoxication
C) Phencyclidine intoxication
D) other hallucinogen related disorder.

DSM5 - Question 52

Phencyclidine; which goes under the names PCP and "Angel dust" is a fast acting compound which can cause severe hallucinations and bizarre behavior. Which of the following symptoms are attributed to phencyclidine use, intoxication, and/or dependence? **[ANSWER: Page 96]**

A) it produces a feeling of separation from mind and body in low doses and in high doses produces a stupor effect and coma.
B) The phencyclidines were produced in the early 1950s as a dissociative type of anesthetic for minor surgery. They began to be abused heavily in the 1960s.
C) although the primary psychoactive effects of PCP last only for a few hours, the total elimination rate from the body can take eight days or longer. Also the hallucinogenic effects in individuals who are vulnerable to this drug can create a persistent psychotic episode resembling schizophrenia.
D) all of the above.

DSM5 - Question 53

Your client presents to the emergency room with the following symptoms: rapid mood changes, increased alertness, excessive talkativeness, hyperactivity, excitement, aggressiveness, anxiety, elevated blood pressure, manic behavior, paranoia, and psychoses. Trouble sleeping (insomnia), loss of energy (malaise), and lack of concentration. What possible substance is responsible for this intoxication?   [ANSWER: Page 96]

A) AB-PINACA, AB-FUBINACA (sold as "Cloud 9," "Relax," or "Crown")
B) MAB-CHMINACA, ADB-CHMINACA (sold as "Mojo," "Spice," "K2," and "Scooby Snax")
C) alpha-pyrrolidinopentiophenone (alpha-PVP), popularly known as "Flakka,"
D) All or any of the above.

DSM5 - Question 54

You are dealing with a client who has been using dip, and tobacco chew for the past five years. They have recently decided to stop using and have not had any product for the last two days. They present to you with anxiety, restlessness, depressed mood, and statements they are not sleeping for the last two nights. This lack of sleep is causing them to have difficulty at the job. They state they have no other mental health issues. Your best possible diagnoses would be...
[ANSWER: Page 97]

A) tobacco dependence
B) tobacco withdrawal
C) tobacco addiction

D) Other unspecified tobacco related disorder.

DSM5 - Question 55

You are doing an assessment on a client who is experiencing depressed mood, dysphoria, difficulty concentrating, nausea, vomiting, and muscle stiffness. They also complained about a headache that "never seems to go away." While gathering information for your psychosocial assessment they indicate they consume 4 to 5 "Red Bulls" every day and often use an over-the-counter product called "5-hour energy". When asked about the last use, they state they stopped about three days ago, because they were concerned that they were not sleeping well. Your best diagnosis would be: **[ANSWER: Page 98]**

A) caffeine intoxication
B) caffeine withdrawal
C) other caffeine induced disorders
D) none of the above

DSM5 - Question 56

Schizophrenia spectrum disorders include abnormalities in one or more of the following five domains: delusions, hallucinations, disorganized thinking, grossly disorganized or abnormal motor behavior, and negative symptoms. Starting with the first domain, delusions are fixed beliefs that are not amenable to change in light of conflicting evidence. These beliefs fall in a variety of themes. You are dealing with the client who believes that certain gestures and comments made by other people are directed at themselves and they are convinced that people are talking about them. Of the following delusional themes this is best described by...

[ANSWER: Page 99]

A) nihilistic delusions
B) grandiose delusions
C) persecutory delusions
D) referential delusions.

DSM5 - Question 57
You are working with a client who is schizophrenic, and they tell you that while they are asleep at night someone comes into the room and rearranges all the bones in their face. Clearly they are experiencing delusions. Because it is clearly implausible and not able to be understood by "same culture peers" and it has not been derived from an ordinary life experience, is deemed as a bizarre delusion. Of the different bizarre delusions, this is best labeled as... **[ANSWER: Page 100]**

A) a delusion of thought insertion
B) a delusion of control
C) a delusion of thought withdrawal
D) none of the above.

DSM5 - Question 58
Hallucinations are perception-like experiences that occur without an external stimulus. They are vivid, clear, and have the full force and impact of a normal perception, and are not under voluntary control. They can occur in any sensory modality; however auditory hallucinations are the most common. Auditory hallucinations are usually experienced as voices, sometimes familiar, sometimes unfamiliar, and they are perceived as distinct from an individual's own thoughts.

Of the following hallucinations, which one is considered to be a problem. [ANSWER: Page 100]

A) a hallucination occurring in a hypnagogic state
B) a hallucination occurring in a clear sensorium
C) a hallucination occurring in a hypnopompic state
D) none of the above.

DSM5 - Question 59
Disorganized thinking, often called a formal thought disorder, is typically inferred from an individual's speech patterns. Individuals may express switching thoughts from one topic to another, answering questions unrelated to the content being asked, speaking in incomprehensible syllables, and a variety of different word patterns that make no sense. You are working with a client who comes to you and their speech pattern appears bizarre and nearly incomprehensible. Upon reading the chart you read the phrase "word salad". What is the specific name for this type of disorganized thinking? [ANSWER: Page 101]

A) derailment or loose association
B) tangential thinking
C) Incoherence
D) aphasia.

DSM5 - Question 60
People with the schizophrenic spectrum disorder often have abnormal motor behavior. This behavior may look like childhood silliness, or go all the way to unpredictability, and/or dangerous agitation. They may have difficulty with any form of goal-directed behavior, and they may not be able

to perform normal activities of daily living. Catatonic behavior is marked by a decrease in reactivity to environmental stimuli. You are working with a client who exhibits excessive and purposeless motor activity that has no obvious or apparent cause. Which type of catatonic behavior are they exhibiting? **[ANSWER: Page 101]**

A) negativism
B) catatonic excitement
C) mutism
D) stupor.

DSM5 - Question 61

An individual diagnosed with schizophrenia may have many associated features that support the diagnosis of the following associated features which are true and appropriate. [DSM5 Page 101]

A) they may display inappropriate affect, dysphoric mood, disturbed sleep pattern, and the lack of interest in eating or even food refusal.
B) while hostility and aggression are associated with schizophrenia, spontaneous or random assault is uncommon. Aggression is more frequent for younger males and for individuals who have a past history of violence, non-adherence to treatment, substance abuse and impulsivity issues.
C) currently there are no radiological, laboratory, or psychometric tests for schizophrenia however there are differences in multiple brain regions as noticed by neurologic imaging and neurological physiology. These differences include different cellular architecture,

reduced overall brain volume, reduce white matter connectivity, and reduced gray matter volume.
D) all of the above.

DSM5 - Question 62
A substance induced or medication induced psychotic disorder is distinguished from a primary psychotic disorder by reviewing the onset, the course, and other factors including drugs of abuse and withdrawal from drugs of abuse. Which of the following are true?

A) Substance or medication induced psychotic disorders arise during or soon after exposure to a medication or after substance intoxication or withdrawal and can persist for weeks.
B) Once initiated, psychotic symptoms due to a substance or medication use will continue, however as soon as the use of the medication, or the abuse of substances end, the psychotic state will end.
C) One consideration in determining psychosis due to substance or medication induced psychotic disorder is an atypical age of onset. We seldom see delusions appear for the first time in persons older than 35 years of age without a known history of a primary psychotic disorder. These delusions de novo should suggest the possibility of a substance induced psychotic disorder. **[Page 103]**
D) A & C

DSM5 - Question 63
You have a client who presented with hallucinations and disorganized speech which lasted for approximately three weeks before going away. All symptoms have been in full

remission for the past six weeks and functioning has returned to pre-symptomatic levels. Your client is 34 years of age and has no other psychotic symptoms, or mental health history. Your best probable diagnosis would be ...
[ANSWER: Page 104]

A) Schizophreniform disorder
B) brief psychotic disorder
C) schizophrenia
D) none of the above

DSM5 - Question 64
You have begun assessing an individual who is diagnosed with a delusional disorder. Unfortunately, your chart review reveals very little data and you are unsure of which subtype of delusion you are dealing with. Your client believes that the manager of the restaurant that he frequents for lunch is secretly in love with him. Several questions uncover the facts that the manager has never talked to your client, never approached your client, and never provided your client with any contact information. When you ask your client about this; he responses, "She looks at me, and I can see it in her eyes." He then goes on to say "I know by the way she runs her fingers to her hair, she is thinking about me sexually." Which of the following delusional subtypes best describes your client? [ANSWER: Page 105]

A) Grandiose type
B) Jealous type
C) Persecutory type
D) Erotomanic type

DSM5 - Question 65

We now know that genetic factors make a strong contribution in determining the risk for schizophrenia. Although most individuals would have been diagnosed with schizophrenia have no family history of psychosis. Which of the following are considered genetic and/or physiological risk factors for schizophrenia?   [ANSWER: Page 106]

A) pregnancy and birth complications with hypoxia
B) greater paternal age
C) perinatal adversities including stress, infection, malnutrition, maternal diabetes
D) all of the above

DSM5 - Question 66

You have been asked to assess the 17-year-old male who was living in a large foster home. He had been caught by the foster parents, three times, sneaking out after dark in order to peek in the window and watch two of his foster sisters undress and get ready for bed. Upon questioning he admits he finds this behavior sexually stimulating and has fantasized about having sex with his two foster sisters. He denies ever attempting to follow through with the fantasy. The foster parents, who have been providing services for many years, are insistent this foster child has a disorder. Your best diagnosis at classifying this behavior would be....
[ANSWER: Page 107]

A) Exhibitionist disorder
B) Voyeuristic disorder
C) Pedophilia disorder
D) none of the above.

DSM5 - Question 67

A second group of paraphilia disorders is the anomalous target preferences. These are paraphilia disorders which are directed either at other human beings, or other nonhuman objects. You are asked a question about a client who has recurrent and intense sexual arousal from either nonliving objects or from a highly specific focus on non-genital body parts. This focus manifests itself as fantasies, urges, and behaviors which are inappropriate and caused the client clinically significant distress. These nonliving objects are not articles of clothing. The best diagnosis for this individual is...
[ANSWER: Page 108]

A) Fetishist disorder
B) Pedophilia disorder
C) Transvestite disorder
D) Frotteuristic disorder

DSM5 - Question 68

Neurocognitive disorders (page 591) in the DSM 5 begin with delirium and include disorders formerly known as Dementia, Alzheimer's, and dementia due to Parkinson's, HIV, or Lewy bodies.

These disorders, given the underlying physical pathology, are very difficult to diagnose. Generally, for the clinical social worker, the awareness of these disorders should be limited to understanding how they differ from each other, and how to interact with an individual diagnosed with these disorders. Assume you are dealing with the patient to his been diagnosed with delirium. Which of the following behaviors might you expect to see? **[ANSWER: Page 110]**

A) a disturbance in attention as manifest by reduced ability to direct, focus, sustain, or shift attention and awareness which results in a reduced orientation to the environment
B) memory deficits, disorientation or a reduced orientation to the environment surrounding the patient.
C) a disturbance of language, visual spatial abilities, or perceptions.
D) all of the above.

DSM5 - Question 69

Paraphilia is defined as any intense and persistent sexual interest other than sexual interest in genital stimulation or preparatory fondling with phenotypically normal, physically mature, consenting adult partners. Paraphilia's are generally broken down into two groups. The first group is called an anomalous activity preference and the second group is called an anomalous target preference.

Of the anomalous activity preferences, these are further subdivided into two groups, the courtship disorders and the algolagnic disorders.

Courtship disorders involve distorted components of human courtship behavior and algolagnic disorders involve pain and suffering.

Based on general knowledge, which of the following is an algolagnic disorder. **[ANSWER: Page 111]**

A) voyeuristic disorder
B) exhibitionist dick disorder
C) sexual sadism disorder
D) none of the above.

DSM5 - Question 70

Gender dysphoria, as described on DSM5 page 451, requires multiple definitions. You are working with an individual who was born as a female and therefore has a gender assignment or a Natal gender of female however they persistently identify themselves as a male. What is the proper designation for this individual according to the DSM5? **[ANSWER: Page 113]**

A) gender nonconforming
B) Transgender
C) general dysphoria
D) transsexual

DSM5 - Question 71

The DSM 5 has pulled together a number of disorders which have somatic symptoms into a new category called somatic symptoms and related disorders. All of the disorders in this section share a common feature: the prominence of somatic symptoms associated with significant distress or impairment. Which of the following is not included in this new category? **[ANSWER: Page 113]**

A) somatic symptoms disorder
B) somatization disorder
C) illness anxiety disorder
D) factitious disorder

DSM5 - Question 72

Somatic symptoms and related disorders have numerous risk and prognostic factors (DSM5 Page 313). Temperamental factors include personality traits with a high negative infinity, for example neuroticism, and comorbid anxiety or

depression. Any of these may make the symptoms and impairment greater. Of the following environmental factors, which factor is not associated with risk or prognostic value.
[ANSWER: Page 115]

A) low social economic status
B) lack of formal education
C) recent stressful life events
D) reported history of sexual abuse during childhood.

DSM5 - Question 73
The illness anxiety disorder entails a preoccupation with having or acquiring a serious, undiagnosed medical illness. Somatic symptoms are either not present or are present but only in mild intensity. A thorough evaluation will fail to identify any serious medical condition that accounts for the concerns. This disorder may sometimes be precipitated by a major life crisis or a serious but ultimately benign threat to an individual's health.

A history of childhood abuse or of a serious childhood illness may allow the individual to develop this disorder later in adulthood. The functional consequences of the illness anxiety disorder are a substantial impairment in physical functioning and health related quality of life.

Health concerns often interfere with interpersonal relationships, disrupt family life, and damage occupational performance.

Which of the following is the best statement to indicate the approximate number of individuals who have a transient form, which is defined as a form with less psychiatric comorbidity and more medical comorbidity, of this disorder?
[ANSWER: Page 116]

A) 1/5 to 1/3
B) 1/2 to 3/4
C) 1/3 to 1/2
D) none of the above.

DSM5 - Question 74

The DSM 5 category of disruptive, impulse control, and conduct disorders include conditions involving problems with self-control of emotions and behaviors. These disorders tend to occur more often in males than females, and tend to first appear in childhood or adolescence. Of the four following diagnostic criteria for an intermittent explosive disorder, which is not accurate. [ANSWER: Page 116]

A) recurrent behavioral outbursts representing a failure to control aggressive impulses as manifest by verbal aggression or physical assaults.
B) the magnitude of aggressiveness expressed during the recurrent outbursts is grossly out of proportion to the provocation or any precipitating psychosocial stressors.
C) the recurrent aggressive outbursts cause marked distress in the individual or impairment in occupational or interpersonal functioning.
D) the recurrent aggressive outbursts are not premeditated but are committed to achieve some tangible objective.

DSM5 - Question 75

Under the DSM 5, somatic symptoms and related disorders you are seeing a client with the following symptoms. They have presented themselves to you and to other people as being injured and impaired. You believe they are falsifying their symptoms and that while you are unsure of the reasoning for this falsification, you believe that there is some reward they are working towards. Which of the following disorders is your best diagnosis? **[ANSWER: Page 117]**

A) conversion disorder
B) factitious disorder
C) unspecified somatic symptoms
D) anxiety illness disorder.

DSM5 - Question 76

The essential feature of post traumatic stress disorder (PTSD) is the development of symptoms which are characteristic for those who have been exposed to one or more traumatic events. New with the DSM 5, you no longer need to chart the emotional reactions to the traumatic event, for example fear, hopelessness, horror, and/or terror. The clinical presentation of PTSD varies widely. Some clients will show fear-based experiences, some will show emotional and/or behavioral symptoms, and others will show anhedonia (inability to experience pleasure) or dysphoric (depressed) symptoms. There are eight sets of criteria for making the diagnosis of PTSD. Which of the following are required for best practice? **[ANSWER: Page 118]**

A) Criterion A: Exposure to actual or threatened death, serious injury or sexual violence.
B) Criterion B: Presence of one (or more) or the intrusive symptoms associated with the traumatic event(s), beginning after the traumatic event occurred.
C) Criterion A & B
D) All Criterion A-H

DSM5 - Question 77

Criterion A: Exposure to actual or threatened death, serious injury or sexual violence; has four sub-parts listed as A1: Directly experiencing the traumatic event(s); A2: Witnessing in person the event(s) as it occurred to others; A3: Learning that the traumatic event(s) occurred to a close family member or close friend; A4: Experiencing repeated or extreme exposure to aversive details of the traumatic event(s). Which of the following events is NOT is not considered to be traumatic enough to warrant a diagnosis of PTSD?
[ANSWER: Page 118]

A) exposure to war as a combatant or a civilian; torture or incarceration as a prisoner of war.
B) threatened or actual physical assault
C) threatened or actual sexual violence
D) None of the above

DSM5 - Question 78

Criterion B: Presence of one (or more) or the intrusive symptoms associated with the traumatic event(s), beginning after the traumatic event occurred; has 5 sub-parts. These are B1: Recurrent, involuntary, and intrusive distressing memories of the traumatic event(s); B2: Recurrent distressing dreams in which the content and/or the effect of the dream are related to the traumatic event(s); B3: Dissociative symptoms (flashbacks) in which the individual feels or acts as if the traumatic event(s) were recurring; B4: Intense or prolonged psychological distress at exposure to internal or external cues that symbolize or resemble an aspect of the traumatic event(s); B5: Marked physiological reaction to internal or external cues that symbolize or resemble an aspect of the

traumatic event(s).
Which of the following events is not considered to be traumatic enough to warrant a diagnosis of PTSD?
[ANSWER: Page 119]

A) a victim of sexual assault seeing someone who resembles their attacker.
B) a victim of war trauma has visual flashes of their combat experiences at different times during the day, with trying to think about the event(s).
C) Lack of sleep due to waking up from dreams in cold sweats and anxiety and then not being able to return to sleep. The dreams are vivid and distressing, although the actual content may not be remembered.
D) All of the above

DSM5 - Question 79
Criterion C is the persistent avoidance of stimuli associated with the traumatic event(s), beginning after the traumatic event(s) occurred. Which of the following best meet this criteria? **[ANSWER: Page 120]**

A) Client states they smoke marijuana in order to relax and avoid past memories.
B) Client refuses to go to the grocery store unless it is after midnight because they feel extremely anxious around a crowd of people.
C) Both A & B
D) B but not A

DSM5 - Question 80

According to Criterion D If the patient exhibits: Negative alterations in cognitions and mood associated with the traumatic event(s), beginning or worsening after the traumatic event(s) occurred, as evidenced by two (or more) of the following... Which of the answers best meets your understanding of Negative Alterations? **[ANSWER: Page 121]**

A) Persistent negative emotional state (e.g., fear, horror, anger, guilt, or shame).
B) Persistent, distorted cognitions about the cause or consequences of the traumatic event(s) that lead the individual to blame himself/herself or others.
C) Feelings of detachment or estrangement from others.
D) All of the above

DSM5 - Question 81

According to the DSM5, Criterion E of the Post Traumatic Stress Disorder is: Marked alterations in arousal and reactivity associated with the traumatic event(s), beginning or worsening after the traumatic event(s) occurred, as evidenced by two (or more) of the following:
Which of the following symptoms are NOT listed with this Criterion? **[ANSWER: Page 121]**

A) Irritable behavior and angry outbursts
B) Reckless or self-destructive behavior.
C) Hyper vigilance
D) Problems with memory

DSM5 - Question 82

According to the DSM5, the final hurdle(s) that need to be crossed in order to appropriately diagnose someone with PTSD are: [ANSWER: Page 122]

A) Duration of the disturbance is less than 1 month.
B) The disturbance causes clinically significant distress or impairment in social, occupational, or other important areas of functioning.
C) The disturbance is attributable to the physiological effects of another medical condition.
D) Both A & C

DSM5 - Question 83
When Diagnosing PTSD in an adult, the diagnosis should be specified as "with delayed expression" if all of the full diagnostic criteria are not met until at least _____ months after the event. [ANSWER: Page 123]

A) 9-12 months
B) 6 months
C) 7-9 months
D) 3-6 months

DSM5 - Question 84
There has been much research on the correlation between suicide and PTSD in recent years. Which of the following is true of the suicide risk associated with PTSD?

[ANSWER: Page 123]

A) PTSD has a neutral correlation with suicide risk

B) PTSD has a positive correlation with suicide risk
C) PTSD has a negative correlation with suicide risk
D) There is no direct correlation between PTSD and Suicide Risk

DSM5 - Question 85
One of the Public Health reasons for studying PTSD is the overall cost to society and the economy. Of the following, which are associated with increased costs of PTSD?
[ANSWER: Page 124]

A) high levels of medical utilization
B) absenteeism from work
C) lower educational and occupational success
D) All of the above

DSM5 - Question 86
The DSM5 has brought many changes to the Anxiety Disorders. The first major change was to move OCD (obsessive-compulsive disorder) and PTSD (posttraumatic stress disorder) into their own respective areas and take them out from under the anxiety disorders. Next for Agoraphobia, Specific Phobia, and Social Anxiety Disorder (Social Phobia), they made the which of the following changes?
[ANSWER: Page 126]

A) a person no longer has to recognize that their anxiety is excessive or unreasonable in order to receive one of these diagnoses.
B) The anxiety now must be "out of proportion" to the actual threat or danger the situation poses, after taking into account all the factors of the environment and situation.

C) The symptoms must also last at least 6 months for all ages.
D) All of the above

DSM5 - Question 87

You are working with a new client who relates the following information: They state they normally have no problems but when certain things "pile up" in their life they are besieged by an intense fear in which their heart races, they experience shortness of breath, they feel dizzy and nauseous and feel like they are going to die. This sensation lasts for 30 - 45 minutes and then slowly abates. They have begun staying in the house more and not going into public as a way of coping. Your BEST diagnostic guess is...
[ANSWER: Page 127]

A) Anxiety disorder
B) Panic Disorder
C) Agoraphobia
D) Medication Induced Anxiety Disorder

DSM5 - Question 88

You are working with a client who begins to experience intense fear and anxiety when they think about going to the grocery store or riding the city bus. When asked about these feelings the client states they are just afraid they will be trapped in the store or on the bus and will not be able to "get out." When they are discussing it they start to breathe heavily and become diaphoretic. The amount of fear they exhibit seems grossly out of proportion to the situation they are discussing. Your best diagnostic statement would be...
[ANSWER: Page 128]

A) Agoraphobia
B) Claustrophobia
C) Panic disorder with emotional distress
D) Generalized Anxiety Disorder.

DSM5 - Question 89
You are dealing with a client who is exhibiting the following symptoms: fear, anxiety, and/or avoidance that is limited to one of the agoraphobic situations and the associated cognitions deal with fear of being directly harmed by the situation itself, using the DSM5 differential diagnosis information would lead to a BEST diagnosis of...
[ANSWER: Page 130]

A) Social Anxiety Disorder
B) Panic Disorder
C) Acute Stress Disorder
D) Specific Phobia, Situational type

DSM5 - Question 90
You are working with a child who exhibits the following behaviors: excessive shyness, fear of social embarrassment, clinging, compulsive traits, negativisms and mild oppositional behavior. They consistently fail to speak in social situations where there is an expectation of speaking. This behavior has been exhibited for approximately 3 months and there are no underlying communication issues noted. Autism is not suspected. Your BEST diagnosis would be:
[ANSWER: Page 131]

A) Panic Disorder
B) Autism Spectrum Disorder

C) Communication disorder not otherwise specified.
D) Selective Mutism

DSM5 - Question 91

For a diagnosis of bipolar I disorder, it is necessary to meet the following criteria for a manic episode. The manic episode may have been preceded by and may be followed by hypomanic or major depressive episodes. In order for a diagnosis for Bipolar 1 Disorder the patient must meet the criteria for a manic episode. The criteria for a Manic Episode require a distinct period of persistently and abnormally elevated, expansive or irritable mood and a persistently and abnormally increased energy, or increased goal-directed activity which lasts for more than a week and for most of the day, almost every day. During the period of this disturbance of mood and increased energy or activity, at least three of the following symptoms are present to a significant degree and represent a noticeable change from their usual behavior. Of the following, which one is NOT a symptom?
[ANSWER: Page 132]

A) Inflated self-esteem or grandiosity.
B) Increased need for sleep
C) More talkative than usual or pressure to keep talking.
D) Flight of ideas or subjective experience that thoughts are racing.

DSM5 - Question 92

The bipolar I disorder criteria is a modern representation of the "classical manic-depressive disorder". In the classical understanding of the nineteenth century "manic-depressive disorder", also known as "affective psychosis", there appears

to be a need for "psychosis" to exist. However, in the DSM5 criteria, a "psychotic episode" is not required to complete the diagnosis. Once a patient meets the criteria in A: A distinct period of abnormally and persistently elevated, expansive, or irritable mood and abnormally and persistently increased goal-directed activity or energy, lasting at least 1 week and present most of the day, nearly every day (or any duration if hospitalization is necessary); and have met three of the following seven criteria in B: Inflated self-esteem or grandiosity; Decreased need for sleep; More talkative than usual or pressure to keep talking; Flight of ideas or subjective experience that thoughts are racing; Distractibility; Increase in goal-directed activity or psychomotor agitation; and/or Excessive involvement in activities that have a high potential for painful consequences. Which of the following complete the diagnostic criteria for the disorder?
[ANSWER: Page 133]

A) The mood disturbance is sufficiently severe to cause marked impairment in social or occupational functioning
B) The mood disturbance is sufficiently severe to necessitate hospitalization to prevent harm to self or others.
C) The episode is not attributable to the physiological effects of a substance (for example a drug of abuse, or medication).
D) All of the above

DSM5 - Question 93
You have been working with a patient who expresses continual dysphoric dreams. They state that upon awakening they quickly become aware of their surroundings. They

describe the dreams as long, very disturbing and fully remembered. They say the dreams often involve a feeling of being chased and trying to avoid capture in order to survive. They state that they have begun to see problems with their work and social life as they are constantly tired, often very sleepy during the day and will occasionally fall asleep in the afternoon at their desk. After some questioning, it is clear they are not using illegal substances or prescription medications which cause nightmares as a side effect. Your BEST diagnosis would be... **[ANSWER: Page 133]**

A) Rapid Eye Movement Sleep Behavior Disorder
B) Nightmare Disorder
C) Sleep terror disorder
D) Bereavement

DSM5 - Question 94

Obsessive-Compulsive Disorder is defined by persistent and recurring thoughts, urges, or images that are intrusive to the patient and unwanted with or without repetitive behaviors or mental acts which the patients feels driven to perform in order to respond to an obsession or the need to apply these actions or rules in a rigid fashion. The patient may also experience preoccupations with mental acts or feel compelled to respond to these preoccupations by using repetitive behaviors or repetitive mental acts. These obsessive-compulsive behaviors are different from normal preoccupations and rituals by their excessive nature and persisting will beyond normal periods or appropriate behavior. You are seeing a patient who seems appropriate during the initial interview but carries a set of worry beads which they keep running through their fingers. When you ask about the beads they say they are "just something they like to hold." Upon further questions they make a statement about their relationship with their father and then begin handling the beads faster and begin talking under their breathe. Upon questioning they tell you that when they have angry feelings about their father they have to repeat the "Serenity Prayer" ten times and count it on the beads. You ask then of there are ever times when they don't have the beads and they laugh and say, "Of course. I never take them into the shower with me. That would be crazy!" Your BEST diagnosis would be: [ANSWER: Page 135]

A) Obsessive-compulsive disorder
B) Trichotillomania
C) Excoriation disorder
D) Obsessive-compulsive and related disorder due to another medical condition

DSM5 - Question 95

Per the DSM5, the characteristic symptoms of OCD are the presence of obsessions and compulsions (Criterion A). Obsessions are repetitive and persistent thoughts (e.g., of contamination), images (e.g., of violent or horrific scenes), or urges (e.g., to stab someone). Importantly, obsessions are not pleasurable or experienced as voluntary: they are intrusive and unwanted and cause marked distress or anxiety in most individuals. The individual attempts to ignore or suppress these obsessions (e.g., avoiding triggers or using thought suppression) or to neutralize them with another thought or action (e.g., performing a compulsion). Compulsions (or rituals) are repetitive behaviors (e.g., washing, checking) or mental acts (e.g., counting, repeating words silently) that the individual feels driven to perform in response to an obsession or according to rules that must be applied rigidly. In the United States, what is the average age of onset of Obsessive-Compulsive Behaviors? **[ANSWER: Page 137]**

A) 10
B) 14
C) 19-20
D) 35

DSM5 - Question 96

In order to diagnose an Acute Stress Disorder [308.3] or [F43.0] the following items must be met. The exposure to actual or threatened death, serious injury, or sexual violation occurs in at least one of the following ways:
By the patient directly experiencing the traumatic event/s or witnessing the event/s as it occurred to others directly.
Also if they learned the event/s occurred to a close family member or friend. If the event/s are actual or threatened death of a family member of friend, the event/s must have been violent or accidental.
The symptoms are generally seen immediately after the trauma event/s but persist for at least 3 days and can last as long as a month.
The patient must also have at least 9 symptoms of distress which begin or become worse after the event/s occurred.
The 9 or more symptoms can span 5 separate categories. Which of the following is NOT one of the 5 categories of distressing symptoms? **[ANSWER: Page 137]**

A) arousal
B) avoidance

C) association
D) negative mood

DSM5 - Question 97

When diagnosing an Acute Stress Disorder [308.3] or [F43.0] and attempting to match symptoms with diagnostic criteria, the following are the intrusive symptoms.
- Recurrent, involuntary, and intrusive distressing memories of the traumatic event/s.
- Recurrent distressing dreams in which the content and/or affect of the dream are related to the event/s.
- Dissociative reactions (e.g., flashbacks) in which the individual feels or acts as if the traumatic event/s were recurring.
- Intense or prolonged psychological distress or marked physiological reactions in response to internal or external cues that symbolize or resemble an aspect of the traumatic event/s.

When diagnosing children, the criteria are slightly different. Of the following which are true? **[ANSWER: Page 138]**

A) In children, repetitive play may occur in which themes or aspects of the traumatic event/s are expressed.
B) In children, there may be frightening dreams without recognizable content.
C) In children, trauma- specific reenactment may occur in play.
D) All of the above

DSM5 - Question 98

When diagnosing Gender Dysphoria without a disorder of

sex development you are referred children from a medical clinic. The onset of cross-gender behaviors is usually between the ages of... [ANSWER: Page 138]

A) 1 and 3
B) 2 and 4
C) 6 and 7
D) 8 and 11

DSM5 - Question 99

The diagnostic criterion for an Inhalant Use Disorder is determined by 10 specific diagnostic symptoms. Remember Inhalant Use Disorder is the ingestion of volatile hydrocarbons which include toxic gases from glues, paints, fuels (like butane and gasoline) and other household chemical compounds. This disorder carries a specifier for the severity of the disorder. Which number of symptoms relates to a severity of Moderate [F18.20]? [ANSWER: Page 139]

A) the presence of 2-3 symptoms
B) the presence of 3-5 symptoms
C) the presence of 4-5 symptoms
D) the presence of 6-10 symptoms

DSM5 - Question 100

The diagnosis of Adult Maltreatment and Neglect Problems are delineated on Page 720 and 721 of the DMS 5. The disorder is divided into 5 separate domains which are Spouse or Partner Violence, Physical; Spouse or Partner Violence, Sexual; Spouse or Partner Neglect; Spouse or Partner Abuse, Psychological; and Adult Abuse by Nonspouse or Nonpartner. Each of these domains are divided into

Confirmed or Suspected. Each of these subdivisions are divided into either an Initial Encounter or Subsequent Encounter.

You are reviewing a situation where the behavior consists of nonaccidental verbal or symbolic acts by one partner that result, or have reasonable potential to result, in significant harm to the other partner. The abused partner refuses to admit the violation and this is the fourth time they have been seen in your clinic for this issue. The best diagnostic label would be? **[ANSWER: Page 139]**

A) Spouse of Partner Violence, Sexual - Confirmed, Subsequent encounter
B) Spouse of Partner Violence, Physical – Suspected, Subsequent encounter
C) Spouse of Partner Neglect, - Suspected, Subsequent encounter
D) Spouse of Partner Violence, Psychological – Suspected, Subsequent encounter.

DSM5 - Answer 1

The correct answer is C

The inclusion of any symptoms would place you in the category of Schizophrenia Spectrum and other Psychotic Disorders. This set of disorders are delineated on page 87 of the DSM 5. (June 2013)

A is INCORRECT

This is one of the disorders in the Schizophrenia Spectrum and other Psychotic Disorders category but has specific criteria.

B is INCORRECT

This is one of the disorders in the Schizophrenia Spectrum and other Psychotic Disorders category but has specific criteria.

D is INCORRECT

This is one of the disorders in the Schizophrenia Spectrum and other Psychotic Disorders category but has specific criteria.

DSM5 - Answer 2

The correct answer is B

Negative symptoms are thoughts, feelings, or behaviors normally present that are absent or diminished in a person with a mental disorder. Anhedonia is the decreased ability to experience pleaser and Alogia is manifested by decreased speech output.

A is INCORRECT

Hallucinations are perception-like experiences that occur

without an external stimulus.

C is INCORRECT
Delusions are fixed beliefs which are not amenable to change in light of conflicting evidence.

D is INCORRECT
Disorganized thinking typically inferred from the individual's speech patterns and is also known as a formal thought disorder.

DSM5 - Answer 3
The correct answer is B
These beliefs are clearly delusions and fall under the specific sub-category of bizarre disillusions because they are clearly implausible, are not understandable to same-culture peers and are not derived from ordinary life experiences

A is INCORRECT
Hallucinations are perception-like experiences that occur without an external stimulus.

C is INCORRECT
Grossly Disorder Behavior is an Abnormal Motor Behavior which can present in a range from child-like silliness to unpredictable agitation.

D is INCORRECT
Negative symptoms are thoughts, feelings, or behaviors normally present that are absent or diminished in a person with a mental disorder.

DSM5 - Answer 4
The correct answer is A
This is the definition of Avolition

B is INCORRECT
This is the definition of Asociality

C is INCORRECT
This is the definition of Alogia

D is INCORRECT
This is the definition of Anhedonia

DSM5 - Answer 5
The correct answer is D
These are all symptoms of a Delusional Disorder.

A is INCORRECT
Brief Psychotic Disorder indicated in Criteria B (DSM 5, Page 94) that the duration of the episode of disturbance is at least 1 day and less than 1 month.

B is INCORRECT
Schizophrenia requires at least two of the 5 Key features of a Psychotic Disorder and for a significant period of time after the onset of the disturbance the level of functioning one or more major areas such as work, self care, etc. is markedly below the level previously achieved.
(DSM 5, Page 99)

C is INCORRECT
Schizophreniform disorder requires at least 2 of the 5 Key

Features of a Psychotic Disorder. These 5 Key Features include Delusions, Hallucinations, Disorganized Speech, Grossly Disorganized or Catatonic Behavior and/or Negative Symptoms.

DSM5 - Answer 6
The correct answer is B
The Criteria include five or more of the following symptoms during the same 2-week period and they must represent a change from previous functioning.
- At least one of the symptoms is (1) depressed mood or (2) loss of interest or pleasure.
- Depressed mood most of the day, nearly every day, as indicated by either subjective report (e.g., feels sad or empty) or observation made by others (e.g., appears tearful). Note: In children and adolescents, can be irritable mood.
- Markedly diminished interest or pleasure in all, or almost all, activities most of the day, nearly every day (as indicated by either subjective account or observation made by others).
- Significant weight loss when not dieting or weight gain (e.g., a change of more than 5 percent of body weight in a month), or decrease or increase in appetite nearly every day. Note: In children, consider failure to make expected weight gains.
- Insomnia or Hypersomnia nearly every day.
- Psychomotor agitation or retardation nearly every day (observable by others, not merely subjective feelings of restlessness or being slowed down).
- Fatigue or loss of energy nearly every day.
- Feelings of worthlessness or excessive or inappropriate

guilt (which may be delusional) nearly every day (not merely self-reproach or guilt about being sick).
- Diminished ability to think or concentrate, or indecisiveness, nearly every day (either by subjective account or as observed by others).
- Recurrent thoughts of death (not just fear of dying), recurrent suicidal ideation without a specific plan, or a suicide attempt or a specific plan for committing suicide.

The symptoms cause clinically significant distress or impairment in social, occupational or other important areas of functioning.

—and—

The symptoms are not due to the direct physiological effects of a substance (e.g., a drug of abuse, a medication) or a general medical condition (e.g., hypothyroidism).

A is INCORRECT
While the symptoms meet the criteria for Major Depressive Disorder, there is no information given which would lead you to believe this event has happened before. The RECURRENT label indicate multiple instances of a depressive episode.

C is INCORRECT
This disorder is new to the DSM 5 and was included for children up to age 18 years who exhibit persistent irritability and frequent episodes of extreme behavioral dyscontrol.

D is INCORRECT
In order for a Major Depressive Episode to be given the MODIFIER "with Mixed Features" there must at least three

manic symptoms; each of which are insufficient to satisfy the criteria for a manic episode.

DSM5 - Answer 7
The correct answer is C
DSM5 has moved to a nonaxial documentation of diagnosis (formally Axes I, II, and III), with separate notations for important psychosocial and contextual factors (formerly Axis IV) and disability (Formerly Axis V). [DSM 5 page 16]

A is INCORRECT
This statement is true.
The DSM5 maintained the approach of the DSM-IV-TR and categorizes the disorders into three distinct clusters. Cluster A are the odd or eccentric disorders, Cluster B are the dramatic, emotional, or erratic disorders and Cluster C are the anxious and fearful disorders. [DSM 5 Page 646]

B is INCORRECT
This statement is true.
While there was a push during development to move the personality disorders from a categorical perspective to dimensional perspective, in the end it was determined to maintain the categorical approach and include the dimensional approach at the end of the manual for study and future consideration.
The dimensional approach states personality disorders are maladaptive variants of personality traits that merge imperceptibly into normality and into one another.

D is INCORRECT
This statement is true.

The DSM5 defines a personality disorder as "an enduring pattern of inner experience and behavior that deviates markedly from the expectations of the individual's culture." [DSM 5 page 645]

DSM5 - Answer 8
The correct answer is D
This is the basic definition of the Schizoid Personality Disorder.

A is INCORRECT
This is the basic definition of the Narcissistic Personality Disorder.

B is INCORRECT
This is the basic definition of the Borderline Personality Disorder.

C is INCORRECT
This is the basic definition of the Dependent Personality Disorder

DSM5 - Answer 9
The correct answer is B
This is FALSE.
The wording in the diagnosis [DSM 5 Page 646] is as follows: The enduring pattern is NOT attributable to the physiological effects of a substance (e.g. a drug of abuse, a medication) or another medical condition.

A is INCORRECT
This is the second (Criteria B) of the 7 criteria for the diagnosis

of a General Personality Disorder.

C is INCORRECT
This is the third (Criteria C) of the 7 criteria for the diagnosis of a General Personality Disorder.

D is INCORRECT
This is the fourth (Criteria D) of the 7 criteria for the diagnosis of a General Personality Disorder.

DSM5 - Answer 10
The correct answer is A
This is a true statement of one of the issues with the differential diagnosis of a personality disorder.

B is INCORRECT
This is a FALSE statement. There is an exclusion criteria stating that the pattern of behavior must NOT have occurred during the course of schizophrenia or a bipolar or depressive disorder with psychotic features.

C is INCORRECT
This is a FALSE statement.
"A personality disorder should be diagnosed only when the defining characteristics appeared before early adulthood." [DSM 5 Page 648]

D is INCORRECT
This is a FALSE statement.
"Personality traits … are diagnosed as a personality disorder only when they are inflexible, maladaptive, and persisting and cause significant functional impairment or subjective

distress." [DSM 5 Page 648]

DSM5 - Answer 11

The correct answer is C

Under DSM–IV, the diagnostic criteria for abuse and dependence were distinct: anyone meeting one or more of the "abuse" criteria within a 12-month period would receive the "abuse" diagnosis. Anyone with three or more of the "dependence" criteria during the same 12-month period would receive a "dependence" diagnosis.

A is INCORRECT
One of the criteria for ALCOHOL ABUSE in DSM0IV was Recurrent alcohol-related legal problems.
—This was not included in the DSM5

B is INCORRECT
Craving or a strong desire or urge to use alcohol.
—This is new to the DSM5

D is INCORRECT
This is true. Under DSM5 Alcohol Use Disorder receives modifiers depending on the number of symptoms present. Modifiers vary from Mild, Moderate to Severe.

DSM5 - Answer 12

The correct answer is A

After full criteria for alcohol use disorder was previously met, none of the criteria for the disorder have been met for at least 3 months but for less than 12 months, WITH the exception of meeting criteria 4.

B is INCORRECT
After full criteria for alcohol use disorder was previously met, none of the criteria for the disorder have been met fat any time during a period of 12 months or longer, WITH the exception of meeting criteria 4.

C is INCORRECT
This is not a modifier used in the DSM5

D is INCORRECT
This modifier is used when is in an environment where access to alcohol is restricted. An Intensive Outpatient Program (IOP) is not a restricted environment. Most residential programs are restricted.

DSM5 - Answer 13
The correct answer is D

A is INCORRECT
Taken alone it is only one of the important characteristics of a substance use disorder (SUD).

B is INCORRECT
Taken alone it is only one of the important characteristics of a SUD.

C is INCORRECT
Taken alone it is only one of the important characteristics of a SUD. [DSM5, Page 483]

DSM5 - Answer 14
The correct answer is D
Omission is due to all of the above statements
[DSM 5 Page 485]

A is INCORRECT
This is only a partial answer.

B is INCORRECT
This is only a partial answer.

C is INCORRECT
This is only a partial answer.

DSM5 - Answer 15
The correct answer is B
The DSM5 eliminated legal criteria from the diagnosis
A is INCORRECT
This s only a partial answer.

C is INCORRECT
This is only a partial answer.

D is INCOORECT
This is only a partial answer.

DSM5 - Answer 16
The correct answer is D
Individuals with this disorder often describe their symptoms as "going crazy" and feeling "time is too fast" or "too slow".

They may also relate fears of irreversible brain damage. They will also often report vague somatic symptoms like lightheadedness and tingling. [DSM 5 Page 302]

A is INCORRECT
The defining characteristics of this disorder is the presence of two or more distinct personality states or an experience of possession. [DSM 5Page 292]

B is INCORRECT
The defining characteristic of this disorder is an inability to recall important autobiographical information that should be successfully stored in long-term memory and would ordinarily be readily available. [DSM 5 Page 298]

C is INCORRECT
This diagnosis described symptoms and characteristics which cause clinically significant distress or impairment, but do not meet the full criteria of any of the other dissociative Disorders [DSM 5 Page 306]

DSM5 - Answer 17
The correct answer is B
This is NOT TRUE. Approximately 50% of adults will experience one lifetime episode of depersonalization/derealization, however, meeting the diagnostic criteria is far more difficult. [DSM 5 Page 303]

A is INCORRECT
This is a true statement

C is INCORRECT
This is a true statement

D is INCORRECT
This is a true statement

DSM5 - Answer 18
The correct answer is D
This describes the suicide risk associated with Dissociative Identity Disorder. [DSM 5 Page 295]

A is INCORRECT
Suicide and other self-destructive behaviors are common in individuals with dissociative amnesia. The risk of suicide is particular great when the amnesia remits suddenly the client is overwhelmed with intolerable memories.

B is INCORRECT
Suicidal risk may be very difficult to assess due to the hypo-emotionality and the client difficulty in focusing and retaining information. The general feeling of "disconnectedness from life" could be weighted as a risk factor or as a protective factor. However, this weighting could rapidly change. Caution is necessary when assessing suicidal risk with clients diagnosed with this disorder.

C is INCORRECT
This category contains no specialized concerns regarding risk assessment for suicide.

DSM5 - Answer 19
The correct answer is B
Mutism in catatonic stupor may suggest dissociative amnesia, but failure of recall is absent. However, other symptoms of

catatonia are present including rigidity, posturing and negativism [DSM 5 Page 301]

A is INCORRECT
Amnesia may occur in the context of a traumatic brain injury (TBI) when there has been an impact to the head or other injury involving rapid movement or displacement of the brain inside the skull.

C IS INCORRECT
In these disorders, memory loss for personal information is usually embedded in cognitive, linguistic, affective, attentional and behavioral disturbances; rather than in autobiographical information.

D IS INCORRECT
These individuals may display complex behavior during seizures and post-ictally (After the seizure) with amnesia which follows, however the amnesia is directly related to the seizure activity.

DSM5 - Answer 20
The correct answer is B.
There are no studies that indicate any genetic link in any aspect of dissociative amnesia.

A is INCORRECT
This is a true statement regarding issues surrounding dissociative amnesia.

C is INCORRECT
This is a true statement regarding issues surrounding

dissociative amnesia.

D is INCORRECT
This is a true statement regarding issues surrounding dissociative amnesia.

DSM5 - Answer 21
The correct answer is B
This is not a word used in the DSM5

A is INCORRECT
The Pretraumatic temporal dimension is broken further into 3 areas which include TEMPERAMENTAL (childhood emotional issues before age 6); ENVIRONMENTAL (lower socioeconomic status, childhood adversity, etc. [DSM 5 Page 277]; and GENETIC & PHYSIOLOGICAL (gender and specific genotypes).

C is INCORRECT
The Peritraumatic temporal dimension includes only ENVIRONMENTAL factors [DSM 5 Page 278]; including the severity (dose) of the trauma, perceived life threat, personal injury, etc. Generally, the greater the magnitude of the trauma, the greater the likelihood of PTSD.

D Is INCORRECT
The Posttraumatic temporal dimension includes TEMPERAMENTAL and ENVIRONMENTAL factors.
Temperamental factors include negative self-evaluation, poor and inappropriate coping mechanisms, and the possible development of an acute stress disorder. The Environmental factors include repeated upsetting reminders, subsequent

adverse life events, trauma related lasses, etc.

DSM5 - Answer 22
The correct answer is D
This set of criteria only apply of the exposure is work-related.
A is INCORRECT
This is a primary criterion for diagnosis with PTSD. It is usually referred to as A1.

B is INCORRECT
This is a primary criterion for diagnosis with PTSD. It is usually referred to as A2.

C is INCORRECT
This is a primary criterion for diagnosis with PTSD. It is usually referred to as A3. It also includes the following: In cases of actual or threatened death of a family member or friend, the events must have been violent or accidental.

The 4th subset under Criteria A is: (A4) Experiencing repeated or extreme exposure to aversive details of the traumatic events. For example, first responders collecting human remains, police officers repeatedly exposed to details of child abuse, etc.

DSM5 - Answer 23
The correct answer is D
All of these are Criteria B diagnostic indicators. Others include involuntary, recurrent distressing memories of the traumatic event and marked physiological reactions to internal or external cues that symbolize an aspect of the trauma.

A is INCORRECT
This is only one of the diagnostic criteria [B4]

B is INCORRECT
This is only one of the diagnostic criteria [B2]

C is INCORRECT
This is only one of the diagnostic criteria [B3]

DSM5 - Answer 24
The correct answer is D
Some of the conditions our soldiers faced and still face in Iraq include the use of the IED. This acronym identifies an Improvised Explosive Device. During the war, the enemy became very proficient at locating and reusing unexploded bombs. These bombs were often hidden in cars abandoned or burned out alongside the road and were inserted into dead dogs, and goats along side the road. Often a spotter would be watching the bomb with the ability to detonate the device with a cell phone when an American Convoy or patrol came by. Our soldiers have suffered many injuries, and watched the death's of their battle-buddies to the IED. It is not abnormal for a returning soldier to have problems driving without '"re-activating this fear."

A is INCORRECT
This is only one of the two correct examples

B is INCORRECT
While there were often spotters nearby, they came in many different shapes, ages, sizes and dress. This answer is too

vague to be useful.

C is INCORRECT
This is only one of the two correct examples

DSM5 - Answer 25
The correct answer is A
The individual's symptoms meet the diagnostic criteria but the gap in memory or an internal refusal to acknowledge the memory or experiences would qualify for this specifier.

B is INCORRECT
This specifier requires persistent or recurrent experiences of feeling detached from oneself, as if you were an observer outside your mental processes.

C is INCORRECT
This specifier would require that the individual would experience the world around them as unreal, dreamlike, distant and/or distorted.

D is INCORRECT
This is used when the full diagnostic criteria are not met until at least 6 months after the event.

DSM5 - Answer 26
The correct answer is B.
This answer describes one of the criteria associated with the eating disorder bulimia 307.51 (F5 0.2).

A is incorrect.

This is one of the diagnostic criteria for anorexia nervosa.

C is incorrect.
This is one of the diagnostic criteria for anorexia nervosa.

D is incorrect.
This is one of the diagnostic criteria for anorexia nervosa.

DSM5 - Answer 27
The correct answer is A.
This is a temperamental factor when dealing with risk and prognosis associated with anorexia nervosa.

B is INCORRECT
This actually an environmental factor used in determining risk for anorexia nervosa

C is INCORRECT
This is actually a genetic and physiological risk and prognostic factor.

D is INCORRECT
This is actually a genetic and physiological risk and prognostic factor.

DSM5 - Answer 28
The correct answer is C
The diagnostic criteria for a rumination disorder, Criteria C, states the eating disturbance does not occur exclusively during the course of anorexia nervosa, bulimia nervosa, binge eating disorder, or avoidant/restrictive food intake disorder. In order to make this diagnosis correctly, you should be able

to see the symptoms, and the behaviors during an eating disorder, and when no eating disorder is present. This diagnosis occurs across multiple domains, but requires constant intervention.

A is INCORRECT
This is part of the diagnostic criteria for rumination disorder.

B is INCORRECT
This one also is part of the criteria for a rumination disorder.

D is INCORRECT
This statement is part of the diagnostic criteria for a rumination disorder.

DSM5 - Answer 29
The correct answer is D
All of these concerns should be reviewed when you are working an individual diagnosed with Bulimia.
IMPORTANT NOTE: IF you are working with a person with Bulimia, you need to have very specialized training and (Best Practice) a supervisor or peer colleague who has special training. This is a disorder that can easily result in client death. It is generally recognized that specialized training is needed.

A is INCORRECT
This is only one of the possible answers

B is INCORRECT
This is only one of the possible answers

C is INCORRECT
This is only one of the possible answers

DSM5 - Answer 30
The correct answer is C.
A sense of lack of control over eating during the episode coupled with eating, in a discrete period of time any amount of food that is definitely larger than what most people would eat in a similar period of time under similar circumstances, is the basic diagnostic criteria for a binge eating disorder. After these two criteria are met, there are a number of other items which need to be evaluated.

A is incorrect.
This is one of the five behaviors which comprise criteria B for the binge eating disorder. This is an important criterion to determine the extent of the binge eating disorder. However, this is not part of the initial two-pronged diagnostic criteria.

B is incorrect.
This is one of the five behaviors which comprise criteria B for the binge eating disorder. This is an important criterion to determine the extent of the binge eating disorder. However, this is not part of the initial two-pronged diagnostic criteria.

D is incorrect.

DSM5 - Answer 31
The correct answer is A.
The paranoid personality disorder is a characterized by a pattern of distrust and suspiciousness, such that other's motives are interpreted as malevolent. It is part of the Cluster

A subcategory.

B is INCORRECT
The avoidant personality disorder is characterized by a pattern of social inhibition, feelings of inadequacy, and hypersensitivity to negative evaluation. It is part of the Cluster C subcategory.

C is INCORRECT
Obsessive-compulsive personality disorder is characterized by a pattern of preoccupation with orderliness, perfectionism, and control. This is part of the Cluster C subcategory.

D is INCORRECT
Dependent personality disorder is characterized by a pattern of submissive and clinging behavior related to an excessive need to be taken care of.
This category is also part of the Cluster C subcategory.

DSM5 - Answer 32
The correct answer is C
Approximately 15% of United States adults have at least one personality disorder.

The prevalence estimates for the different clusters suggest that approximately 5.7% of individuals diagnosed with the Cluster A personality disorder will also have a personality disorder from the other cluster subcategories.

Approximately 1.5% of those diagnosed with a Cluster B subcategory of personality disorder will meet the diagnostic criteria for another personality disorder in another subcategory.

Approximately 6.0 percent of patients diagnosed with a Cluster C subcategory personality disorder will show the diagnostic criteria for a personality disorder in one of the other cluster subcategories.

A is INCORRECT
This is not the percentage approximated by the national epidemiological survey

B is INCORRECT
This is not the percentage approximated by the national epidemiological survey

D is INCORRECT
This is not the percentage approximated by the national epidemiological survey

DSM5 - Answer 33
The correct answer is D
The pervasive characteristics of this presentation are a pattern of distrust and suspiciousness, with the motives of people interacting with him being regarded as malevolent or damaging. He clearly meets criteria A1, "suspects, without sufficient basis, that others are exploiting or deceiving."; and criteria A4 "reading hidden meanings or threatening meanings in benign remarks or events." He also meets criteria A6 "perceives attacks on his character and reputation that are not apparent to others and is quick to react angrily and counter attack."
Also, it should be noted, that his description of his parents

describe a person with paranoid personality disorder and one may assume that the traits of the parents have been modeled, on some level, by the son.

A is INCORRECT
The pattern of behavior does not include a disregard for or violation of the rights of others.

B is INCORRECT
There is no data to indicate a pattern of acute discomfort in close relationships, cognitive perceptual distortions, and for eccentricities of behavior.

C is INCORRECT
There is no pattern in the data indicate excessive emotionality and attention seeking behavior.

DSM5 - Answer 34
The correct answer is B.
This individual shows a pattern of disregard for, and violation of, the rights of others. He has legal involvement, and appears to be willing to lie in order to get his needs met.

A is INCORRECT
The pattern here does not show an acute discomfort in close relationships, cognitive perceptual distortions, or eccentricities of behavior.

C is INCORRECT
The pattern here is not submissive and clinging behavior related to an excessive need to be taken care of.

D is INCORRECT
There is no pattern of excessive emotionality and attention seeking behavior.

DSM5 - Answer 35
The correct answer is A
There is a pattern of cognitive and perceptual distortions and eccentricity of behavior. Magical thinking creates another layer to this drama.

B is INCORRECT
There is no pattern of disregard for and or violation of the rights of others.

C is INCORRECT
There is no pattern of submissive or clinging behavior related to an excessive need to be taken care of.

D is INCORRECT
There is no pattern of excessive emotionality and attention seeking.

DSM5 - Answer 36
The correct answer is A
This is the primary presentation of the borderline personality disorder. It includes black/white thinking, frantic efforts to avoid being alone and quickly changing moods.

B is INCORRECT
There is no pattern of disregard for and or violation of the rights of others.

C is INCORRECT
There is no pattern of submissive or clinging behavior related to an excessive need to be taken care of.

D is INCORRECT
There is no pattern of excessive emotionality and attention seeking.

DSM5 - Answer 37
The correct answer is C
There is a pattern of submissive or clinging behavior related to an excessive need to be taken care of.

A is INCORRECT
There is no pattern of cognitive and perceptual distortions and eccentricity of behavior.

B is INCORRECT
There is no pattern of disregard for and or violation of the rights of others.

D is INCORRECT
There is no pattern of excessive emotionality and attention seeking.

DSM5 - Answer 38
The correct answer is B
There is a pattern of hypersensitivity, poor interactional social skills and an overall pattern of avoiding social situations when they are not completely comfortable.

A is INCORRECT

There is no pervasive pattern of distrust and suspiciousness, and no indication the motives of people interacting with them are being regarded as malevolent or damaging.

C is INCORRECT
Obsessive-compulsive personality disorder is characterized by a pattern of preoccupation with orderliness, perfectionism, and control.

D is INCORRECT
Dependent personality disorder is characterized by a pattern of submissive and clinging behavior related to an excessive need to be taken care of.

DSM5 - Answer 39
The correct answer is D
There is a pattern of excessive emotionality and attention seeking. They enjoy being the center of attention and are feel uncomfortable when ignored.

A is INCORRECT
There is no pattern of cognitive and perceptual distortions and eccentricity of behavior.

B is INCORRECT
There is no pattern of disregard for and or violation of the rights of others.

C is INCORRECT
There is no pattern of submissive or clinging behavior related to an excessive need to be taken care of.

DSM5 - Answer 40

The correct answer is D

Schizoid personality disorder is a cluster A disorder, which makes it part of the odd and peculiar personality disorders. It only occurs in approximately less than 1 percent of the population.

Its characteristics include not having close personal relationships and choosing to remain detached from others in society. Persona with this disorder often engage in introverted activities and arrange their life in such a way that even their choices of professions require very minimal interaction with others. They will often take on a job position even if their abilities far exceed the job criteria These individuals appear to view themselves as bystanders instead of as an active member in society.

A is INCORRECT
There is no pattern of cognitive and perceptual distortions and eccentricity of behavior.

B is INCORRECT
There is no pattern of disregard for and or violation of the rights of others.

C is INCORRECT
There is no pattern of submissive or clinging behavior related to an excessive need to be taken care of.

DSM5 - Answer 41

The correct answer is D
Borderline personality disorder, like ALL other disorders is subject to differential diagnosis. Substance abuse and

addiction can present as Borderline personality disorder and if the addiction began during the patient's teenage years, it is very difficult to separate out this disorder from addictive behavior. As a general rule, I never diagnose a Borderline personality disorder when there is active addiction.

A is INCORRECT
This is an accurate statement about differential diagnosis.

B is INCORRECT
This is an accurate statement about differential diagnosis.

C is INCORRECT
This is an accurate statement about differential diagnosis.

DSM5 - Answer 42
The correct answer is C
This statement is not true. Schizotypal personality disorder is thought to be slightly more common in males than females.

A is INCORRECT
This is a true statement. Borderline Personality Disorder is diagnosed in families at a ratio of 3:1. The reason for this is unclear and may be confounded by societal perceptions. I once heard a clinician say "the antisocial personality disorder is the borderline diagnosis for males." I am not sure I agree with this, however, it is thought provoking due to male-female socialization issues.

B is INCORRECT
This statement is true in regards to Schizoid personality

disorder.

D is INCORRECT
This statement is true in regards to obsessive-compulsive personality disorder.

DSM5 - Answer 43
The correct answer is D
All of these symptoms and traits are found in the substance abuse arena.

A is INCORRECT
This answer is incomplete.

B is INCORRECT
This answer is incomplete.

C is INCORRECT
This answer is incomplete.

DSM5 - Answer 44
The correct answer is B
This statement is NOT true when discussion Opioid Use Disorders. HIV and Hepatitis C are prevalent in injection use due to blood-to-blood contact, however, they are not prevalent in opioid use of prescription abuse, primarily to the the oral self-administration of the pill form of the drug.

A is INCORRECT
This is a TRUE STATEMENT regarding Opioid Use Disorder Comorbidity

C is INCORRECT
This is a TRUE STATEMENT regarding Opioid Use Disorder Comorbidity

D is INCORRECT
This is a TRUE STATEMENT regarding Opioid Use Disorder Comorbidity

DSM5 - Answer 45
The correct answer is D
The prevalence rates between injection use and prescription (pill) use is very different. HIV and HEP-C are very common in IV opioid abuse; however, they are not prevalent in prescription drug use. This is because of the "vector of transmission"; oral administration versus intravenous administration.

A is INCORRECT
The following is a true statement about opioid use: individuals with an opioid use disorder are at increased risk of developing mild to moderate depression which can meet the criteria for persistent depressive disorder and in some cases major depressive disorder.

B is INCORRECT
The following is a true statement about opioid use: insomnia is common both in opioid use disorder and upon withdraw from opioid use.

C is INCORRECT
The following is a true statement about opioid use:

in opioid use disorder the individual may present with symptoms of slurred speech, attention impairment, memory impairment, and drowsiness.

DSM5 - Answer 46
The correct answer is D

Tolerance is defined as either a necessary increase in use to achieve the same effect, or a markedly diminished effect when using the same amount.

For example; six months ago your client began abusing Adderall by taking one pill every 12 hours, now they have to take 1 pill every 4 hours to "feel the same high" or they used to take one pill every 12 hours and they "felt great", but now that one pill appears to have no effect on their feelings.

A is INCORRECT
This answer is not correct because it is only half of the definition of tolerance.

B is INCORRECT
This answer is not correct. I am aware of no substance of abuse where continued use of the same amount gives an increase in effect.

C is INCORRECT
This answer is not correct because it is only half of the definition of tolerance.

DSM5 - Answer 47
The correct answer is D.
All three of these are part of the 11 diagnostic criteria for alcohol use disorder.

A is incorrect
This is only part of the correct answer, and requires the other two parts for a complete answer.
[a great deal of time is spent in activities necessary to obtain alcohol, use alcohol, or recover from its effects.]
B is incorrect
This is only part of the correct answer, and requires the other two parts for a complete answer.
[important social, occupational, or recreational activities are given up or reduced because of alcohol use.]

C is incorrect
This is only part of the correct answer, and requires the other two parts for a complete answer.
[there is a persistent desire or unsuccessful efforts to cut down or control alcohol use.]

DSM5 - Answer 48
The correct answer is A
The twelve-month prevalence of alcohol use disorder among adults decreases in middle-age. It is greatest among individuals 18-29 years old and lowest among individuals aged 65 years and older.

A is INCORRECT
Prevalence rates are not lowest among individuals age 45 to 65 years old.

C is INCORRECT
Prevalence rates are among individuals 18 to 29 years' old

D is INCORRECT
This one should be obvious by now.

DSM5 - Answer 49
The correct answer is D
All of these are problematic behavioral or physiological changes associated with alcohol intoxication.

A is INCORRECT
This answer is incorrect because it is incomplete. Impaired judgment and belligerence are also specific to Criterion B.

B is INCORRECT
This answer is incorrect because it is incomplete. Mood labiality and belligerence are also specific to Criterion B.

C is INCORRECT
This answer is incorrect because it is incomplete. Impaired judgment and mood labiality are also specific to Criterion B.

DSM5 - Answer 50
The correct answer is D
All of these are part of the societal cost of alcohol use disorder. However, these are not the only problems. The list of concerns, issues and problems could fill a book in its own right.

A is INCORRECT
This answer is only partially correct. 40% of individuals in the United States experience and alcohol related adverse event at sometime in their life; and 55% of all fatal driving events include and are accounted for by alcohol use are also

part of the answer.

B is INCORRECT
This answer is only partially correct. one in five intensive care unit in missions in urban hospitals is related to alcohol use.; and 55% of all fatal driving events include and are accounted for by alcohol use are also part of the answer.

C is INCORRECT
This answer is only partially correct. 40% of individuals in the United States experience and alcohol related adverse event at sometime in their life; and one in five intensive care unit in missions in urban hospitals is related to alcohol use are also part of the answer.

DSM5 - Answer 51
The correct answer is C
This description is classic phencyclidine intoxication. People on this substance can produce amazing feats of strength and have been reported to continue fighting and/or running after they have broken bones which would incapacitate a normal person.

A is INCORRECT
This answer is not specific enough. There are a number of hallucinogens which cause a variety of effects, and this set of behaviors is almost totally indicative of Phencyclidine use.

B is INCORRECT
Amphetamine intoxication has a very different presentation.

D is INCORRECT

This is not specific enough a label.

DSM5 - Answer 52
The correct answer is D
All of these are symptoms are related to Phencyclidine intoxication of abuse. While is is relatively rare to see this drug currently, its ability to be manufactured locally always allows it to comeback into street use. It also looks very similar to "Spice" and "Ecstasy" intoxication which is growing in seriousness daily.

A is INCORRECT
This is only a partial answer

B is INCORRECT
This is only a partial answer

C is INCORRECT
This is only a partial answer

DSM5 - Answer 53
The correct answer is D

A is INCORRECT
because it is a partial answer.
Additional information. * It is sold as a liquid in eyedropper bottles and often used with vaporizing devices—e-cigarettes or "hookah pens." Numerous hospitalizations in Michigan prompted the Macomb County Health Department to issue an emergency warning and ban on the sale of these drugs, which are reported to cause hallucinations, aggressive behavior, racing heartbeat, drowsiness, and vomiting.

B is INCORRECT
Because it is a partial answer.
Additional information. * This chemical has resulted in over 150 hospital visits in Baton Rouge and Lafayette, LA in October 2014, prompting the governor to ban the drug in that state. It is reported to cause severe agitation, anxiety, and paranoia; raised heartbeat and blood pressure; nausea and vomiting; muscle spasms, seizures, and tremors; intense hallucinations and psychotic episodes, including suicidal fixations and other harmful thoughts.

C is INCORRECT
Because it is a partial answer.
Additional information. *Alpha-PVP is chemically similar to other synthetic cathinone drugs popularly called "bath salts," and takes the form of a white or pink, foul-smelling crystal that can be eaten, snorted, injected, or vaporized in an e-cigarette or similar device. Vaporizing, which sends the drug very quickly into the bloodstream, may make it particularly easy to overdose. Like other drugs of this type, alpha-PVP can cause a condition called "excited delirium" that involves hyperstimulation, paranoia, and hallucinations that can lead to violent aggression and self-injury. The drug has been linked to deaths by suicide as well as heart attack. It can also dangerously raise body temperature and lead to kidney damage or kidney failure.
*http://www.drugabuse.gov/drugs-abuse/emerging-trends#Cloud_9 (Accessed September 25, 2015)

DSM5 - Answer 54
The correct answer is B.

These are all symptoms of tobacco withdrawal coded as 292.04 code or F17.203. The diagnostic criteria are: daily use of tobacco for at least several weeks, abrupt cessation of tobacco use followed within 24 hours four or more of the following symptoms: irritability, frustration and/or anger; anxiety; difficulty concentrating; increased appetite; restlessness; depressed mood; and insomnia. These symptoms cause clinically significant distress or impairment in social, occupational, or other important areas and they are not attributed to another medical condition or better explained by another mental disorder.

A is INCORRECT
Tobacco Dependence has a very different set of symptoms

C is INCORRECT
This is not a DSM5 diagnosis. This is a layman's phrase.

D is INCORRECT
This has a completely different set of diagnostic symptoms.

DSM5 - Answer 55
The correct answer is B.
All of these symptoms are related to withdrawal from caffeine. We generally think of caffeine as a benign substance. However, in moderate to large doses it can cause psychological problems including insomnia, hypervigilance, and even paranoid ideations. One of the current issues with caffeine, is the ease with which it can be obtained, as an increasing number of products include caffeine. We are also seeing problems with alcohol use and caffeine because the "energy drinks" are being mixed with alcohol in party

atmosphere which often allow the user to consume more alcohol than is safe.

A is INCORRECT
Intoxication looks different from withdrawal. It looks much similar to psychosis.

C is INCORRECT
This is a catch all diagnosis which is used when enough information can not be gathered. There is plenty of information in question to formulate a diagnosis.

D is INCORRECT
The answer is above.

DSM5 - Answer 56
The correct answer is D
Referential delusions are the belief that certain gestures, comments, environmental cues and social interactions are directed at oneself. Everything references the person with the delusion.

A is INCORRECT
Nihilistic delusions revolve around the idea that a major catastrophe will occur.

B IS INCORRECT
Grandiose delusions are when a person he or she has exceptional abilities, wealth or fame.

C is INCORRECT
Persecutory delusions are the believe that one is going to be

harmed or harassed by an individual or organization.

DSM5 - Answer 57
The correct answer is B
Delusions of control are the belief that one's body or actions are being manipulated by or acted upon by outside forces and the person involved does not have control over their own movements or body.

A is INCORRECT
Delusions of thought insertion are the belief that someone outside of you are putting thoughts and ideas into your brain. This often is thought to be the work of aliens or intelligence agencies, by the person suffering from schizophrenia spectrum disorder.

C IS INCORRECT
Delusions of thought withdrawal are the belief that someone else, outside of one's own body, is removing thoughts and ideas from your mind or brain.

D is INCORRECT
Obviously

DSM5 - Answer 58
The correct answer is B
In order to be classified as a hallucination, they must occur in a clear sensorium.

A is INCORRECT
A hypnagogic state occurs when you are falling asleep. During this state you may have many experiences, however

these are not considered hallucinations.

C is INCORRECT
A hypnopompic state occurs when you are waking up from sleep. During this state you may have many experiences, however these are not considered hallucinations.

D is INCORRECT
Obviously

DSM5 - Answer 59
The correct answer is C
Incoherence is linguistic disorganization that resembles receptive aphasia and is often referred to as "word salad."

A is INCORRECT
Derailment or loose association occurs when the individual switches from one topic to another, quickly and without a pattern.

B is INCORRECT
Tangential thinking occurs when an individual responds to questions obliquely or with completely unrelated responses.

D is INCORRECT
Aphasia is the name given to a collection of language disorders caused by damage to the brain.

DSM5 - Answer 60
The correct answer is B
Catatonic excitement (which seems like an oxymoron) is defined as excessive and purposeless motor activity that has

no obvious or apparent cause.

A is INCORRECT
Negativism is a resistance to instructions.

C is INCORRECT
Mutism is a complete lack of verbal responses.

D is INCORRECT
Stupor is a complete lack of motor responses.

DSM5 - Answer 61
The correct Answer is D
These are all signs and symptoms of schizophrenia.

A is INCORRECT
This is only part of the answer.
Individuals with schizophrenia may display inappropriate affect, dysphoric mood, disturbed sleep pattern, and the lack of interest in eating or even food refusal.

B is INCORRECT
This is only part of the answer.
Hostility and aggression are associated with schizophrenia; spontaneous or random assault is uncommon. Aggression is more frequent for younger males and for individuals who have a past history of violence, non-adherence to treatment, substance abuse and impulsivity issues.

C is INCORRECT
This is only part of the answer.
Currently there are no radiological, laboratory, or

psychometric tests for schizophrenia however there are differences in multiple brain regions as noticed by neurologic imaging and neurological physiology. These differences include different cellular architecture, reduced overall brain volume, reduce white matter connectivity, and reduced gray matter volume.

DSM5 - Answer 62

The correct answer is D

Both A and C are true when discussing medication induced or substance abuse induced psychosis.

A is INCORRECT

While Substance or medication induced psychotic disorders arise during or soon after exposure to a medication or after substance intoxication or withdrawal and can persist for weeks, this is only a partial answer for the question.

B is INCORRECT

Once initiated, psychotic symptoms due to a substance or medication use will continue, and can persist for weeks afterward. Symptoms may not immediately subside.

C is INCORRECT

While, we seldom see delusions appear for the first time in persons older than 35 years of age without a known history of a primary psychotic disorder, this is only a partial answer. You should always consider an atypical age of onset to be a possible psychosis due to substance or medication inducement.

DSM5 - Answer 63

The correct answer is B.

This is an episode of a brief psychotic disorder. (DSM 5 Page 94) The client displays delusions, hallucinations, or disorganized speech, grossly disorganized and catatonic behavior. The duration of the event lasts for more than one day but for less than a month with an eventual return to premorbid levels of functioning. Also this disturbance is not better explained by a major depressive disorder, bipolar disorder with psychotic features, or another psychotic disorder. These behaviors are not attributed to the physiological effects of a substance use, medication use, or other medical condition. This disorder can be marked with four specific specifiers.

The first specify is "with marked stressors"; the second is "without marked stressors"; the third is "with postpartum onset"; and the fourth is "with catatonia".

A is INCORRECT

One of the primary differences between the schizophreniform disorder and a brief psychotic disorder is that a schizophreniform disorder lasts for at least one month less than six months. It has three specifiers which include with "with good prognostic features"; "without good prognostic features"; and "with catatonia.)

C is INCORRECT

The diagnosis of Schizophrenia requires a great deal of information over a long period of time. Generally, the symptoms must be present for more than six months, and can have multiple episodes and multiple periods of remission.

D is INCORRECT
This is obvious.

DSM5 - Answer 64
The correct answer is D

The central theme of this type of delusion is another person is in love with the individual. This conviction is held with little or no proof. Often the object of this delusion is in a higher social position, a famous individual, someone who is in a higher position at work. However, they can be a complete stranger. Often times the individual will go to great lengths to try to contact the object of this delusion.

A is INCORRECT.
The central theme of the grandiose delusion is the belief or conviction that the individual has some great talent, insight, or has made an important discovery. This person believes that their talent and their contribution is far greater than reality would have you believe.

B is INCORRECT.
In this type of delusion, the central theme is an unfaithful partner. This belief is often arrived at without any cause or is based on incorrect inferences or small amounts of "evidence". Often times this imagine infidelity causes anger, and conflict in the relationship. An example of a small detail might be one partner who arrives home one night with their shirt tail untucked, their tie undone or their makeup smudged.

C is INCORRECT
This particular delusion revolves around the individuals

believe they are being conspired against, cheated on, spied on, followed, poisoned, maligned maliciously, harassed for no reason, or obstructed from being able to obtain a long-term or life goal. Small slights are often exaggerated and become the focus of the delusional system. The affected individual may often engage in repeated attempts to obtain satisfaction for the slight by legal or administrative action.

DSM5 - Answer 65
The correct answer is D.
All of the above.
There is a belief that there is a large spectrum of risk alleles, both common and rare. Each allele contributing only a small fraction of the total population variance of schizophrenia.

A is INCORRECT
While pregnancy and birth complications with hypoxia are associated with higher rates of schizophrenia, they are not the only things associated with greater risk. This is a partial answer

B is INCORRECT
This is also only a partial answer.
The greater the age of the father the higher the possibility of schizophrenia in the offspring.

C is INCORRECT
This is also a partial answer. Any perinatal adversities, including stress, infection, malnutrition, maternal diabetes, and other medical conditions have been linked to an increase in schizophrenia. However, the vast majority of offspring with these risk factors do not develop schizophrenia. The

development of schizophrenia is a very complicated and complex process and is currently unknown to psychiatric science.

DSM5 - Answer 66
The correct answer is D.
While this discussion has aspects of voyeurism in it, it does not meet the criteria of a voyeuristic disorder on two specific accounts. First, there is the lack of indication of a specific time the behavior has been going on. Second, the age of the individual involved does not meet the necessary criteria.

A is INCORRECT
An exhibitionist disorder deals with a recurrent or intense sexual arousal, over a period of at least six months, from the exposure of one's genitals to an unsuspecting person, and is manifested by fantasies, urges, and behaviors. The individual has also acted upon the sexual urges with a non-consenting person and the sexual urges have caused clinically significant distress in the individual acting upon these feelings.

B is INCORRECT
A Voyeuristic disorder occurs over a period of at least six months and deals with recurrent and intense sexual arousal from observing an un-expecting person who is naked, in the process of disrobing, or is engaged in sexual activity and is manifested by fantasies, urges, and behavior. While the six-month period should not be considered absolute, a definite length of time should be involved.
The individual who has acted upon the sexual urges feels clinically significant distress or impairment from acting on these feelings. The individual experiencing the arousal or

acting on these urges is at least 18 years of age.

It is accepted that adolescence and puberty are a time of increased sexual curiosity and activity. In order to keep from pathologizing behavior which may be normal sexual interest and normal behavior during puberty/adolescence, the minimum age for diagnosis is 18.

C is INCORRECT
The pedophilia disorder deals with a six-month time period of recurrent or intense sexual arousal dealing with fantasies, sexual urges or behaviors involving activity with a pre-pubescent, or prepuberty child, generally considered to be less than 13 years of age.
The individual has acted on the sexual urges and the sexual urges or fantasies cause marked distress in the individual.
The individual is at least 16 years of age and there's at least five years' age difference between the individual and the child or children that they are aroused by.

DSM5 - Answer 67
The correct answer is a.
This situation describes of fetishistic disorder. Where, over a period of at least six months there were recurrent and intense sexual arousal from the use of nonliving objects or a highly specific focus on non-genital body parts. This is manifest as fantasies, urges, or behaviors, and causes clinically significant distress or impairment in social, occupational, or other important areas of functioning.

It is important to note that these fetishistic objects are not limited to articles of clothing used in cross-dressing or are not devices specifically designed for the purpose of tactile genital stimulation (for example a vibrator). There are three specifiers for the use with the fetishistic disorder. They are body parts, nonliving objects, or other.

B is INCORRECT
Pedophilia disorder involves recurrent or intense sexual arousal or sexually arousing fantasies, sexual urges, or behaviors which involve sexual activity with a prepubescent child.
Generally, this is considered a child under the age of 13 years. However, it defines a child who does not have secondary sexual characteristics i.e. pubic hair or breasts. This diagnosis also requires that the individual has either acted on the sexual urges or the sexual urges and fantasies cause distress and interpersonal difficulty.

There is also a requirement that the individual is at least 16 years of age and there is at least five years' age difference between the individual and the child or children involved in this actually arousing fantasies.

Understanding this definition would mean that an 18-year-old who was fantasizing about a prepubescent 13-year-old may well be diagnosed as a pedophilia disorder, however a 20-year-old fantasizing about a pubescent 15-year-old may not meet the criteria for pedophilia disorder

C is INCORRECT.
The Transvestite disorder requires recurrent or sexually intense arousal for at least a period of six months from cross-dressing as manifest by fantasies, urges, or behaviors.

These fantasies, urges, or behaviors cause clinically significant distress or impairment in social, occupational, or other important areas of functioning.

It is important to note that cross-dressing, or sexual arousal from cross-dressing does not meet the threshold of a disorder if the behavior, fantasies, or urges do not cause clinically significant distress or impairment.

D is INCORRECT

This disorder is one of the anomalous activity disorders. Unlike the other three disorders described which are anomalous target preferences. This disorder involves recurrent or intense sexual arousal, happening for a period of at least six months, from touching or rubbing against a non-consenting person as manifest my fantasies, urges, or behaviors.

This individual has acted upon the sexual urges with a non-consenting person or the urges and fantasies cause clinically significant distress or impairment.

While Frotteuristic acts, including uninvited sexual touching or rubbing against another individual may occur in up to 30% of adult males in the general population, only 10 to 14% of these acts would meet the criteria for diagnosis of Frotteuristic disorder.

DSM5 - Answer 68

The correct answer is D.

All of these are diagnostic criteria for delirium. These also include a disturbance which develops over a short period of time, usually from several hours to several days, and represents a clear change from baseline attention and awareness.

The inattention and awareness can fluctuate in severity during the day, becoming more problematic in the evening, or in early morning. You must also rule out these disturbances is being caused by another medical condition, or substance intoxication or withdrawal.

An example of another medical condition would be a urinary tract infection in a geriatric adult. Octogenarians with a urinary tract infection often present in a state of delirium, however as soon as the infection is treated with antibiotics, the delirium clears.

B is INCORRECT
This is a partial answer.

A is INCORRECT
This is a partial answer.

C is INCORRECT
This is also a partial answer.

DSM5 - Answer 69

The correct answer is C

The algolagnic disorders involve pain and suffering. There are two of these disorders. They are the sexual masochism disorder and the sexual sadism disorder. In the sexual masochism disorder the individual, over a period of at least six months, receives recurrent and intense sexual arousal from the act of being humiliated, beaten, bound, or otherwise made to suffer, as manifested by fantasies and urges. These fantasies and urges cause clinically significant distress or impairment in social functioning.

In the sexual sadism disorder, over a period of six months the individual experiences intense sexual arousal from the physical or psychological suffering of another person as manifested by fantasies or urges.

The individual has acted on the sexual urges with a non-consenting person or the sexual urges and fantasies cause clinically significant distress or impairment in social or occupational functioning.

It is important to note that the sexual sadism disorder requires the sadistic acts or urges occurring within non-consenting person. If both adults are consenting, then you may have actions which are sexually sadistic and rise to the level of sexual sadism, but do not rise to the level of being a disorder.

B is INCORRECT
Exhibitionism is an activity. And therefore it belongs to the group of anomalous activity preferences. It is also an interactive behavior so as part of the subgroup of courtship disorders, although it is a distorted example of courtship.

A is INCORRECT
Voyeurism is an activity. Therefore, it too is part of the anomalous activity preferences. Voyeurism involves a very distorted relationship and is therefore part of the subclass of courtship disorders.

D is INCORRECT
This should be obvious.

DSM5 - Answer 70

The correct answer is B

Transgender refers to a broad spectrum of individuals who transiently or persistently identify themselves with a gender different from their natal or born gender.

A is INCORRECT

Gender nonconforming is an alternative description for gender – atypical. Which refers to somatic features or behaviors which are not statistically typical of individuals with the same assigned gender in a given society or historical era.

C is INCORRECT

Gender dysphoria is a generally descriptive term which refers to an individual's affect of or cognitive discontent with their assigned gender.

D IS INCORRECT

Transsexual denotes an individual who seeks or has undergone a social transformation from male to female or female to male and also may have, but does not require somatic transition by cross sex hormone treatment or genital surgery, also known as sex reassignment surgery.

DSM5 - Answer 71

The correct answer is B.

This disorder is a DSM-IV disorder and was altered with the new DSM5. This disorder was considered to be part of the somatoform disorders. It was determined to be a confusing set of disorders with a great deal of overlap, and lack of clarity about the individual boundaries of the diagnosis.

A is INCORRECT

The somatic symptoms disorder is one of the new DSM 5 disorders. The basic diagnostic criteria include one or more somatic symptoms that are distressing or result in significant disruption of daily life. This is coupled with excessive thoughts, feelings, or behaviors related to the somatic symptoms and one or more of the following: disproportionate and persistent thoughts about the seriousness of one symptoms, persistently high level of anxiety about health, or excessive time and energy devoted to the symptoms or health concerns. Generally, the somatic symptoms should be present for at least six months

C is INCORRECT

The illness anxiety disorder is a DSM 5 somatic symptoms and related disorder diagnosis. It includes preoccupation with having or acquiring a serious illness combined with somatic symptoms which are either not present, or only mild. There is a preoccupation that is clearly disproportionate to the symptomatology. The individual also show a very high level of anxiety about health.

D is INCORRECT

The factitious disorder involves the falsification of physical or psychological signs or symptoms or induction of injury or disease associated with the attempt to deceive. The individual usually present themselves to others is being ill, impaired, or injured. This behavior although deceptive, is evident even in the absence of obvious external rewards. The behavior is not better explained by another mental disorder.

DSM5 - Answer 72

The correct answer is D.

A reported history of sexual abuse or other childhood adversity is one of the course modifiers of the somatic symptoms disorder. It is not one of the environmental risk factors. This should be obvious because a history of sexual abuse is not an environmental factor.

A is INCORRECT
Lower social economic status is a risk and prognostic factor for this disorder. This is one of the many reasons why the social worker clinician should complete a very thorough psychosocial assessment.

B is INCORRECT
Lower levels of education are associated with greater risk and poor prognostic outcome of a somatic symptom disorder. Many disorders have a correlation with lower economic status and lower amounts of education. This is once again why a complete Psychosocial Assessment is very important. The more data you gather, the more you are able to provide a clear picture for treatment planning and the eventual health of the client.

C is INCORRECT
Recently experienced stressful life events increase the probability of developing a somatic disorder and decrease the prognosis for remission of the disorder. Generally somatic disorders are exacerbated by many environmental factors.

DSM5 - Answer 73
The correct answer is C.
One-third to one-half of persons suffering from this disorder have the transit form.

A is INCORRECT
This ratio is too small

B is INCORRECT
This ratio is too large.

D is INCORRECT
This is obvious.

DSM5 - Answer 74
The correct answer is D.
The recurrent aggressive outbursts are not premeditated and they are not committed to achieve a tangible objective such as money, power, intimidation. They seem to be outside of the conscious or voluntary control of the patient.

A is INCORRECT.
This is actually one of the appropriate diagnostic criteria for an intermittent explosive disorder. More information can be found on DSM 5 page 467.

B is INCORRECT
One of the problems with treating someone with this disorder, is the lack of insight and the lack of understanding how their behavior is perceived by others.

C is INCORRECT.

This answer is correct. This is one of the diagnostic criteria and can be further explored using a psychosocial assessment.

DSM5 - Answer 75

The correct answer is B

These are the basic symptoms of a factitious disorder. Even though you are unsure of the reward, the creation of false symptoms clearly falls into this disorder. It should be noted that the factitious disorder has another side, known as factitious disorder imposed on another. This disorder occurs when a person falsifies an illness in another person, usually a child, in order to be perceived as the savior for helping the child.

The older term for this was Munchausen syndrome or Munchausen syndrome by proxy.

A is INCORRECT

The conversion disorder does not involve falsification of symptoms. The symptoms may appear very real. However, the evidence of incompatibility between the symptoms and the neurological or medical condition of the patient is obvious.

C is INCORRECT

The unspecified somatic symptoms and related disorder applies to presentations in which the symptoms are characteristic of a somatic disorder and cause clinically significant distress or impairment however they do not meet the full criteria for any of the disorders in this category.

D is INCORRECT

The illness anxiety disorder is predicated on the

preoccupation of having or acquiring a serious illness. If somatic symptoms are present they are only mild in intensity, or if another medical condition is present, this disorder deals with an excessive or disproportionate preoccupation with the real disorder.

DSM5 - Answer 76
The correct answer is D
Best practice is to cover all 8 criterion and document in your notes the behaviors, thoughts, or statements of the client as it pertains to the specific aspects of each diagnosis.
Nothing is more frustrating than having a chart with a diagnosis of PTSD and there no stressors, events, or issues noted and no way to know where to start the therapeutic process

A is INCORRECT
This is only a partial answer and will not qualify as best practice.

B is INCORRECT
This is only a partial answer and will not qualify as best practice.

C is INCORRECT
This is only a partial answer and will not qualify as best practice.

DSM5 - Answer 77
The correct answer is D
These are all events which are considered to be traumatic and would support a diagnosis of PTSD. It is important to note

that if the experiences are indirect, for example learning about the trauma happening to someone else, the other person must be a close relative or a close friend and the event must have been violent or accidental. A 'death due to natural circumstances' is not considered sufficient.

A is INCORRECT
These are an example of traumatic events which support a PTSD diagnosis.

B is INCORRECT
These are an example of traumatic events which support a PTSD diagnosis. Specific examples might be physical attack, robbery, mugging, childhood physical abuse, etc.)

C is INCORRECT
These are an example of traumatic events which support a PTSD diagnosis. Specific examples may well include forced sexual penetration, alcohol/drug facilitated sexual penetration, abusive sexual contact, sexual trafficking, forced prostitution, etc.

DSM5 - Answers 78
The correct answer is D
All of these are events which meet the level of intensity for Criterion B.

A is INCORRECT
This would be an example of Criterion B5.
Marked physiological reaction to internal or external cues that symbolize or resemble an aspect of the traumatic event(s).

B is INCORRECT
This would be an example of Criterion B1.
Recurrent, involuntary, and intrusive distressing memories of the traumatic event(s).

C is INCORRECT
This would be an example of Criterion B2.
Recurrent distressing dreams in which the content and/or the effect of the dream are related to the traumatic event(s).

DSM5 - Answer 79
The correct answer is C
Both of these meet the criteria for PTSD.

A is INCORRECT
This is a partial answer. This meets the criteria C1: Avoidance of or efforts to avoid distressing memories, thoughts, or feelings about or closely associated with the traumatic event(s). [DSM 5 Page 271]

B is INCORRECT
This is a partial answer.
This meets criteria C2: Avoidance of or efforts to avoid external reminders (people, places, conversations, activities, objects, situations) that arouse distressing memories, thoughts, or feelings about or closely associated with the traumatic event(s). [DSM 5 Page 271]

D is INCORRECT
This only provides one-half the correct response.

DSM5 - Answer 80

The correct answer is D

All of these are examples of meeting Criterion D. Others are:
- Inability to remember an important aspect of the traumatic event(s) (typically due to dissociative amnesia and not to other factors such as head injury, alcohol, or drugs).
- Persistent and exaggerated negative beliefs or expectations about oneself, others, or the world (e.g., "I am bad," "No one can be trusted," "The world is completely dangerous," "My whole nervous system is permanently ruined").
- Markedly diminished interest or participation in significant activities.
- Persistent inability to experience positive emotions (e.g., inability to experience happiness, satisfaction, or loving feelings).

A is INCORRECT
This is only a partial answer

B is INCORRECT
This is only a partial answer

C is INCORRECT
This is only a partial answer

DSM5 - Answer 81

The correct answer is D
Criterion E recognizes "problems with concentration" but not "problems with memory."

A is INCORRECT
This is a behavior recognized under criterion E.

"Irritable behavior and angry outbursts (with little or no provocation) typically expressed as verbal or physical aggression toward people or objects.

B is INCORRECT
This is a behavior recognized under criterion E. Reckless or self-destructive behavior.

C is INCORRECT
This is a behavior recognized under criterion E. Hypervigilance.

The other three behaviors under this criterion are:

-Exaggerated startle response.
-Problems with concentration.
-Sleep disturbance (e.g., difficulty falling or staying asleep or restless sleep).

DSM5 - Answer 82
The correct answer is B
The disturbance causes clinically significant distress or impairment in social, occupational, or other important areas of functioning.

A is INCORRECT
Duration of the disturbance (Criteria B, C, D, and E) is more than 1 month.

C is INCORRECT
The disturbance is not attributable to the physiological effects of a substance (e.g., medication, alcohol) or another medical

condition.

D is INCORRECT
This answer is obvious.

DSM5 - Answer 83
The correct answer is B
Specify if: With delayed expression: If the full diagnostic criteria are not met until at least 6 months after the event (although the onset and expression of some symptoms may be immediate).

A is INCORRECT
This is too long of a delay.

C is INCORRECT
This delay period is also too long.

D is INCORRECT
This delay period is too short.

DSM5 - Answer 84
The correct answer is B
PTSD is associated with suicidal ideation and suicide attempts (Sareen et al. 2005; Sareen et al. 2007), and presence of the disorder may indicate which individuals with ideation eventually make a suicide plan or actually attempt suicide (Nock et al. 2010).

A is INCORRECT
A neutral correlation would be the same as D, which would indicate that the presence of one has no effect on the presence

of the other. Much like the color of an umbrella would have no effect on its ability to keep you dry.

C is INCORRECT
If this were correct, it would mean the more severe the PTSD symptoms, the less risk of suicide, and vice versa.

D is INCORRECT
Please see the answer for A.

Sareen J, Houlahan T, Cox B, Asmundson GJ: Anxiety disorders associated with suicidal ideation and suicide attempts in the National Comorbidity Survey. J Nerv Ment Dis 193(7):450–454, 2005

Sareen J, Cox BJ, Stein MB, et al: Physical and mental comorbidity, disability, and suicidal behavior associated with posttraumatic stress disorder in a large community sample. Psychosom Med 69(3):242–248, 2007

Nock MK, Hwang I, Sampson NA, Kessler RC: Mental disorders, comorbidity and suicidal behavior: results from the National Comorbidity Survey Replication. Mol Psychiatry 15(8):868–876, 2010

DSM5 - Answer 85
The correct answer is D
All of these issues are associated with PTSD.

A is INCORRECT
This is only a partial answer. Research indicates that there is a rather large economic cost which correlates to the higher

levels of occupational and social impairment caused by PTSD. There is also an increased utilization of medical resources which increase societal costs as well.
(Arnow et al. 2000; Kartha et al. 2008)

B is INCORRECT
This is only a partial answer. Higher levels of absenteeism are associated with PTSD.

C is INCORRECT
This is only a partial answer. Lower educational and lower occupational success are correlated with PTSD.

(Olatunji et al. 2007; Sayer et al. 2011; Schnurr et al. 2009)

****

Arnow BA, Hart S, Hayward C, et al: Severity of child maltreatment, pain complaints and medical utilization among women. J Psychiatr Res 34(6):413–421, 2000

Kartha A, Brower V, Saitz R, et al: The impact of trauma exposure and post-traumatic stress disorder on healthcare utilization among primary care patients. Med Care 46(4):388–393, 2008

Olatunji BO, Cisler JM, Tolin DF: Quality of life in the anxiety disorders: a meta-analytic review. Clin Psychol Rev 27(5):572–581, 2007

Sayer NA, Carlson K, Schnurr P: Assessment of functioning and disability in individuals with PTSD, in Clinical Manual for the Management of Posttraumatic Stress Disorder. Edited by Benedek D, Wynn GH. Washington, DC, American Psychiatric Publishing, 2011, pp 255–287

Schnurr PP, Lunney CA, Bovin MJ, Marx BP: Posttraumatic stress disorder and quality of life: extension of findings to veterans of the wars in Iraq and Afghanistan. Clin Psychol Rev 29(8):727–735, 2009

DSM5 - Answer 86

The Correct answer is D
All of these changes have been made to the Anxiety disorders.

A is INCORRECT
It is a partial answer.
Often insight is lacking in individuals with an anxiety disorder as they may misattribute their fears to a variety of other causes. They may also downplay the severity of their fears.

B is INCORRECT
It is a partial answer.
There now has be an objection understanding on the diagnostician's part that the anxiety is "out-of-proportion" to the perceived situation. This change was brought about based on evidence that individuals with such disorders often overestimate the danger in "phobic" situations.

C is INCORRECT
It is a partial answer.
This change is intended to help minimize over-diagnosis of occasional fears.

DSM5 - Answer 87

The correct answer is B

These symptoms are the hallmark of a Panic Disorder. The scenario described above is a rather extreme example due to the physiological symptoms and the "feeling they are going to die."

The primary diagnostic features of a Panic disorder start with an abrupt surge and have at least 4 of the following symptoms during their surge: Palpitations, pounding heart, or accelerated heart rate; sweating; trembling or shaking; sensations of shortness of breath or smothering; feelings of choking, chest pain or discomfort, nausea or abdominal distress, feeling dizzy, unsteady, light-headed, or faint, chills or heat sensations; paresthesia (numbness or tingling sensations); derealization (feelings of unreality) or depersonalization (being detached from oneself); fear of losing control or "going crazy."; and fear of dying.

A is INCORRECT

The Anxiety disorder has a broader set of symptoms and presents in a more pervasive format.

C is INCORRECT

Agoraphobia has a rather specific set of symptoms which are seen when in public, large crowds or open spaces. You should generally think of agoraphobia as a rather specific subset of panic disorder.

D is INCORRECT

No medication was discussed in the question.

Additional information:
Always gather enough information in your psychosocial assessment to determine if the behavior is related to the physiological effects of a substance; for example, drug abuse, or from prescribed medications which can have side-effects.

DSM5 - Answer 88

The correct answer is A

This is classic Agoraphobia.

The criteria include fear or anxiety when faced with at least 2 of the following 5 situations: Using Public transportation, being in public places, being in enclosed spaces, being in a crowd and being outside alone. When this is paired with a fear and avoidance of these situations because they "might not be able to escape" or "help might not be available" if they develop panic symptoms and this fear/anxiety is clearly out of proportion to the situation, and the anxiety/fear cause clinically significant distress or dysfunction, agoraphobia is the general diagnosis.

B is INCORRECT

This is a more specific response to a very specific situation. This would be diagnosed as a phobia.

C is INCORRECT

This is not a diagnosis. Panic Disorder is a diagnosis, but when you add, with emotional distress it is no longer an appropriate DSM5 diagnosis.

D is INCORRECT

Generalized Anxiety Disorder is a rather large category which contains anxiety and fear as symptoms, but is much less specific in regards to the actual triggers or situations. Think 'Generalized" means broad in scope.

Additional Information:
Prevalence:
- Approximately 1.7% of adolescents and adults have a diagnosis of agoraphobia every year.
- Females are twice as likely as males to experience agoraphobia
- While Agoraphobia may occur in childhood, incidence peaks in late adolescence and early adulthood
- Prevalence rates do not appear to vary systematically across cultural/racial groups

Development and Course
- The majority of individuals with panic disorder show signs of anxiety and agoraphobia before the onset of panic disorder.
- In two-thirds of all cases of agoraphobia, initial onset is before age 35 years.
- There is a substantial incidence risk in late adolescence and early adulthood.
- First onset in childhood is rare.
- The overall mean age at onset for agoraphobia is 17 years,
- The age of onset without preceding panic attacks or panic disorder is 25–29 years
- The course of agoraphobia is typically persistent and chronic.
- Complete remission is rare (10%), without treatment.
- The more severe the agoraphobia, the greater the decrease in full remission and the rates of relapse/chronicity increase.
- There is an increase in co-morbid disorders such as

depressive disorders, substance use disorders, and personality disorders.
- Co-morbid disorders complicate the course of agoraphobia.
- The clinical features are usually consistent across the client's lifespan.
- Over time the type of agoraphobic situations which trigger fear, anxiety, or avoidance have been known to vary.
- In children, being alone outside the home is the most frequently feared situation.
- In older adults, shopping, standing in line, and being in open spaces is the most frequently feared situation.

DSM5 - Answer 89
The correct answer is D
Differentiating agoraphobia from situational specific phobia is challenging because they share specific symptoms, characteristics and criteria.

In general, a "Specific phobia, situational type", should be used if the fear, anxiety, and/or avoidance are limited to only one of the agoraphobic situations.

Also, the cognitive ideations will be different. In agoraphobia, the cognitions revolve around fear of panic-like symptoms and/or embarrassing or incapacitating symptoms, while in the specific phobia the fear is more directly related to the situation itself. For example, a fear of heights is linked to a fear of death by falling.

A is INCORRECT
In a social anxiety disorder the differential is focused on fear of being negatively evaluated rather than on situational

clusters that trigger fear, anxiety, or avoidance.

B is INCORRECT

If the avoidance behaviors are associated with panic attacks and do not extend to avoidance of two or more agoraphobic situations, the diagnosis should be Panic disorder.

C is INCORRECT

Acute stress disorder can be differentiated from agoraphobia by examining whether the fear, anxiety, or avoidance extend to two or more agoraphobic situations. If they do not, then agoraphobia is the wrong diagnosis.

Additional Information:

In major depressive disorder, the individual may avoid leaving home because of apathy, loss of energy, low self-esteem, and anhedonia. This avoidance is unrelated to fears of panic-like symptoms. It is also unrelated to incapacitating or embarrassing symptoms.

DSM5 - Answer 90

The correct answer is D

This is the diagnostic criteria for Selective Mutism. It is a rare disorder with sampling showing the rate of appearance range from 0.03% to 1%.

The disorder usually starts before age 5, however, is is not often diagnosed until the child enters the school system.

There does not seem to be any difference between gender, race or ethnicity in its presentation.

A is INCORRECT

There is no indication of any panic issues in the information presented.

B is INCORRECT
The question clearly states Autism is not suspected.

C is INCORRECT
The question clearly states there is no underlying communication issues other than the selective mutism

DSM5 - Answer 91
The correct answer is B.
The actual criteria are: Decreased need for sleep. (e.g., feels rested after only 3 hours of sleep).

A is INCORRECT
This is one of the criteria for the Bipolar 1 Disorder
-- Inflated self-esteem or grandiosity.

C is INCORRECT
This is one of the criteria for the Bipolar 1 Disorder
-- More talkative than usual or pressure to keep talking.

D is INCORRECT
This is one of the criteria for the Bipolar 1 Disorder
-- Flight of ideas or subjective experience that thoughts are racing.

Additional information:
The remaining criteria for Bipolar 1 Disorder are:
-- Distractibility (i.e., attention too easily drawn to unimportant or irrelevant external stimuli), as reported or

observed.
-- Increase in goal-directed activity (either socially, at work or school, or sexually) or psychomotor agitation (i.e., purposeless non-goal-directed activity).
-- Excessive involvement in activities that have a high potential for painful consequences (e.g., engaging in unrestrained buying sprees, sexual indiscretions, or foolish business investments).

Also: If the patient presents with an IRRITABLE mood, then they need to exhibit four of these behaviors during a Manic Phase, rather than the normal three.

DSM5 - Answer 92
The correct answer is D
All of these symptoms are criteria for the Bipolar 1 Disorder.

A is INCORRECT
This is a partial answer.
This is one of the criteria for the disorder.

B is INCORRECT
This is a partial answer.
This is one of the criteria for the disorder.

C is INCORRECT
This is a partial answer.
This is one of the criteria for the disorder.

DSM5 - Answer 93
The correct answer is B
Nightmare Disorder   The diagnostic criteria for this

disorder are:
- Repeated occurrences of extended, extremely dysphoric, and well-remembered dreams that usually involve efforts to avoid threats to survival, security, or physical integrity and that generally occur during the second half of the major sleep episode.
- On awakening from the dysphoric dreams, the individual rapidly becomes oriented and alert.
- The sleep disturbance causes clinically significant distress or impairment in social, occupational, or other important areas of functioning.
- The nightmare symptoms are not attributable to the physiological effects of a substance (e.g., a drug of abuse, a medication).
- Coexisting mental and medical disorders do not adequately explain the predominant complaint of dysphoric dreams.

A is INCORRECT
The differential diagnosis for Rapid Eye Movement Sleep Behavior Disorder includes:
- Complex motor activity during frightening dreams.
- age of prevalence is late middle age and gender is predominantly males
- often includes violent dream enactments
- can include a history of nocturnal injuries
- is generally controllable by medication

C is INCORRECT
The differential diagnosis for Sleep terror disorder includes:
- both disorders include awakenings or partial awakenings.
- both disorders include with fearfulness and autonomic activation

- nightmares typically occur later in the night, during REM sleep.
- dreams are vivid, story-like, and clearly recalled.
- they involve mild autonomic arousal and sometimes complete awakenings.
- Sleep terrors typically arise in the first third of the night during stage 3 or 4 NREM sleep.
- they produce no dream recall or images without an elaborate story-like quality.
- they lead to partial awakenings that leave the patient confused and disoriented.
- they leave the patient only partially responsive.
- they include substantial autonomic arousal.
- they often involve amnesia of the dream event upon awakening in the morning.

D is INCORRECT
The differential diagnosis for Bereavement includes:
- Dysphoric dreams during bereavement typically involve loss and sadness.
- They are often followed by self-reflection and insight.
- They are often not distressing upon awakening

DSM5 - Answer 94
The correct answer is A
This presentation of symptoms includes both obsessive behaviors (fingering the worry beads) and obsessive thoughts (monitoring thoughts for angry thoughts about his father) but also compulsions (the need to repeat the Serenity Prayer a specific number of times). The obsessions are time consuming (always carrying the beads and fingering them), they are not easily attributed to the effects of substance abuse,

or prescribed medications, and there is no indication of another mental disorder which is responsible for them.

B is INCORRECT

Trichotillomania's essential feature is the recurring" pulling out" of one's own hair. It is often called the "hair-pulling disorder". This pulling can occur almost anywhere on the human body but is most often concentrated on the scalp, eyebrows, and eyelids. Less commonly seen is pulling hair from face, pubic region or peri-rectal region. This behavior can occur with brief episodes or sustained periods of time. It can be episodic or continual for years.

C is INCORRECT

Excoriation disorder, also known as "skin-picking" is defined as the recurring picking at one's own skin. Most commonly the face, hands and arms are the site of the picking. Picking can be concentrated on healthy skin or small skin irregularities (pimples, callouses, scabs). Additionally, they may exhibit skin rubbing, lancing, biting or squeezing behaviors. This behavior can take up several hours each day.

D is INCORRECT

Obsessive-compulsive and related disorder due to another medical condition is diagnosed when the obsessive behavior is due to another medical condition, rather than a reaction to substance abuse or an adverse reaction to prescription medications or over-the-counter formulations. The scenario above does not contain any information regarding drugs or medications.

DSM5 - Answer 95
The correct answer is C
The average age of onset of Obsessive-compulsive behaviors is 19.5

A is INCORRECT
According to Ruscio, et al 2010, approximately one-quarter or 25 percent of males have an onset before 10 years of age.

B is INCORRECT
According to Kessler et al 2005, approximately one-quarter or 25 percent of all cases have an onset by 14 years of age.

D is INCORRECT
According to Ruscio et al 2010, & Kessler et al 2005 onset after 35 years of age is unusual. However, it can occur.

Kessler RC, Chiu WT, Demler O, et al: Prevalence, severity, and comorbidity of 12-month DSM-IV disorders in the National Comorbidity Survey Replication. Arch Gen Psychiatry 62(6):617–627, 2005

Ruscio AM, Stein DJ, Chiu WT, Kessler RC: The epidemiology of obsessive-compulsive disorder in the National Comorbidity Survey Replication. Mol Psychiatry 15(1):53–63, 2010

DSM5 - Answer 96
The correct answer is C
Association is not one of the distressing symptoms of the Acute Distress Disorder. However, disassociation is.

A is INCORRECT
Arousal is one of the five categories of symptoms which are required to diagnosed Acute Stress Disorder.

B is INCORRECT
Avoidance is one of the five categories of symptoms which are required to diagnosed Acute Stress Disorder.

D is INCORRECT
Negative Mood is one of the five categories of symptoms which are required to diagnosed Acute Stress Disorder.

Additional information:
The 5 categories are intrusion, negative mood, dissociation, avoidance, and arousal.

DSM5 - Answer 97
The correct answer is D
All of these are qualifiers which pertain to children when diagnosing this disorder.

A is INCORRECT
This is a partial answer. All the criteria are true.

B is INCORRECT
This is a partial answer. All the criteria are true.

C is INCORRECT
This is a partial answer. All the criteria are true.

DSM5 - Answer 98
The correct answer is B

This age range is correlated to the developmental stage when children begin developing gendered behaviors and gendered interests. (DSM 5 Page 455)

A is INCORRECT
This is pre-gender awareness

C is INCORRECT
This is past gender development interest and into the development of relationship skills outside the family structure.

D is INCORRECT
This stage is much too late. This is a time when development centers around groups, membership and social belonging.

DSM5 – Answer 99
The correct answer is C
Moderate is defined as 4-5 symptoms.
(DSM 5 Page 534)

A is INCORRECT
This is the definition of Mild Severity [F18.10]

B is INCORRECT
This does not correlate with any severity marker.

D is INCORRECT
This is the definition of Severe [F18.20]

DSM5 – Answer 100
The correct answer is D

Spouse of Partner Violence, Psychological – Suspected, Subsequent encounter. There is no physical force mentioned, it is suspected but not confirmed and this is not the first time.

A is INCORRECT

Spouse of Partner Violence, Sexual - Confirmed, Subsequent encounter. There is no forced or coerced sexual acts mentioned, is is not confirmed, but it is a subsequent encounter.

B is INCORRECT

Spouse of Partner Violence, Physical – Suspected, Subsequent encounter. There is no physical force mentioned, is is unconfirmed and it is a subsequent encounter.

C is INCORRECT

Spouse of Partner Neglect, - Suspected, Subsequent encounter. There is no mention of an egregious act or omission in the past year by one partner that deprives the dependent partner of basic needs and thereby results, or has the reasonable potential to result, in physical or psychological harm to the dependent partner

Made in United States
Troutdale, OR
04/26/2024

19471562R00086